MY CANYONLANDS

MY CANYONLANDS
I had the freedom of it.
by KENT FROST

ABELARD-SCHUMAN

London   New York   Toronto

© Copyright 1971 by Kent Frost
Library of Congress Catalogue Card Number: 76-139292
ISBN 0 200 71775 8

LONDON	NEW YORK	TORONTO
Abelard-Schuman	Abelard-Schuman	Abelard-Schuman
Limited	Limited	Canada Limited
8 King St. WC2	257 Park Ave. So.	228 Yorkland Blvd.

An **Intext** Publisher

Printed in the United States of America

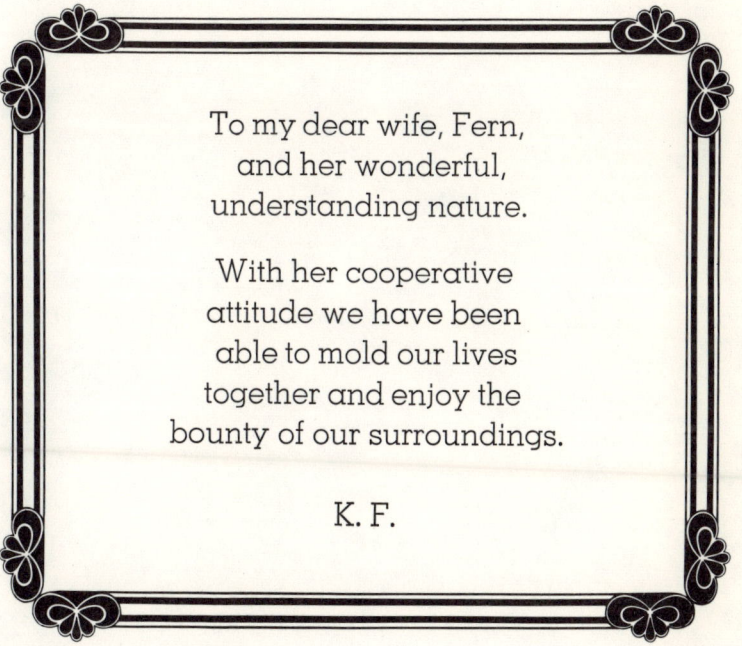

To my dear wife, Fern,
and her wonderful,
understanding nature.

With her cooperative
attitude we have been
able to mold our lives
together and enjoy the
bounty of our surroundings.

K. F.

R01144 55160

CONTENTS

Chapter	Page No.
Introduction	9

Part I. THE EXPANDING MAP

1.	13
2.	16
3.	18
4.	27
5.	34
6.	41
7.	47
8.	53
9.	60
10.	71
11.	75
12.	81
13.	95
14.	98

Part II. THE DWINDLING WILDERNESS

15.	111
16.	122
17.	128
18.	134
19.	143
20.	153

INTRODUCTION

With wonder, I count our fleet of four-wheel-drive vehicles parked around our Monticello home.

I stand, cushion-footed, on our springy lawn—my wife can make garden grass grow that thick in this dry land. I see her through our picture window. It frames Fern at her desk, writing. For her the window frames an outside portrait of our good friend, Blue Mountain.

Fern is answering the letters that come every week from travelers across the United States and around the world who want to take trips with us. I marvel that this sleek scene is the direct result of my homesteader's childhood. Inaugurated by necessity, continued by preference, I have had the rare experience of being a frontiersman in the twentieth century. Here I am, with a foot in each era, finding that both soils have been good for my growth.

Although San Juan County was an outpost, a remote community, its face was firmly, if unknowingly, set towards supermarkets and tile bathrooms. I merely set mine in an opposite direction and had the good fortune to live in a place where I could move that other way.

The other way was into the canyon wilderness, wild, lonely, and mighty . . . the racing rivers and lofty mountains . . . the eerie deserts . . . the secret canyons. Their big silence still awes me. Alone, in my earliest explorations, it used to frighten me. My loudest yell was scattered like raindrops on slickrock. A soft sound was magnified into unexpected importance. But hard desert country tempers the spirit to correspond with the elements.

It drew me then. It draws me still. I must always be off somewhere . . . up a mountain, into a canyon, down a river. I have to get out where I almost freeze to death in the winter. Then I can appreciate my own fireside.

Or perhaps I start thinking about some mysterious canyon I've never explored. Curiosity gnaws at me. Finally I take a pocketful of provisions, find a way in, and hike until I'm too weary for another step. The ground I know best is what my feet touch or what I sleep on, coverless, beside a fire. Scanty fare that sustains life is my excitement in "living off the land." I have done everything I could to make myself strong and able to cope with the elements.

One thing that appears clear to me now is that the moments of adventure—for the most adventurous—are widely separated by long periods of hard work. Perhaps it's best that way.

The demands of life here are harsh. People earn their livings in odd ways. Ingenuity still counts. Most folks find it necessary to do three things at once for income—they run a farm, ranch, or store, hold a civic office, then find a third job for cash. Not moonlighting so much as trilighting.

The rewards must be great to hold us all here—though certainly they are not the usual ones. We seem to appreciate having plenty of space in which to move around and time without frantic pressure to think about what we're doing.

Some of this land is still wild, but not for much longer. Here is where the last frontier is crumbling away.

I am glad I had the freedom of it in such a special way and that I have been able to introduce others to its beauty.

I would not have had my life any other way.

K. F.

PART 1
The Expanding Map

Bluff with its schoolhouse and lazy horses.

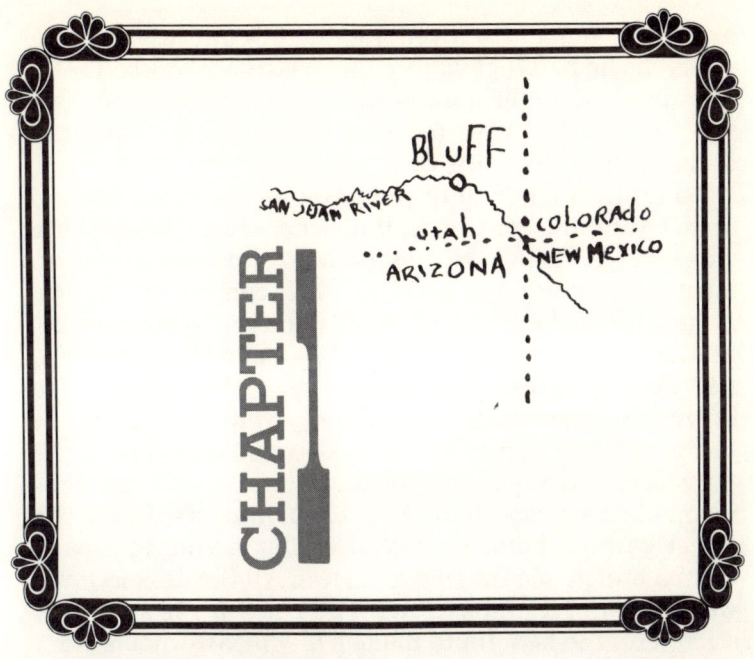

When I was six my map of the world was Bluff, Utah. Bluff was a town in San Juan County, Utah, in the Four Corners area. Sixty inhabitants lived in 25 houses, strung around a grassy street between the San Juan River and the redrock walls of high canyons that end there. The schoolhouse I attended is now the city jail, but I could have told you it always was. I managed to take one day out of every week to climb the sandhills and red rimrock. I would go around to the Indian camps, too. There were many Navajos and Paiutes living near us, and I could always find some at the stores.

One afternoon there was an Indian more impressive than the rest, standing with a blanket around his shoulders.

"Who's he?" I whispered to one of the big boys.

"Joe Bishop. His son was killed at Blanding," he answered, referring to Posey's Rebellion in nearby Blanding in 1925, the last Indian uprising in the United States.

After that I used to stand off under a cottonwood tree

and stare at Joe. He loved a game of coin toss, pulling out coins he had tucked into his massive silver belt. The men pitched silver dollars to a stake, the nearest coin winning all. I always felt glad when Joe won and the dollars returned to his belt.

Sometimes a bunch of men around the store worked up to a jumping contest, Indians and whites. Broadjump was the favorite. Hop-skip-and-jump was another. Squaw wrestling was popular, with contestants on the ground, arms locked, and heads pointing in opposite directions. At the count of three they locked legs, the winner finally pulling the other over. When they were brimming over with energy they would all suddenly jump on their horses and race down Main Street.

I was eating my lunch one day when an exciting clatter made me drop my fork and run outdoors. Down the street came a horse in a wild gallop, trying to escape from a bunch of cans tied to its tail. All the dogs in town were chasing it and barking. The gang at the store had stirred up the bedlam to make a sleepy afternoon more interesting. They did it whenever they wanted to get rid of a horse they didn't like. It was never one of theirs.

In Spring, the big boys started going down to the San Juan River to fish. I followed them. I guess my sisters kept a sharper eye and tighter hand on my brother Alfred than they did on me. They managed to keep him in school more of the time. I soon learned to fish for myself. Sometimes, I would bring back a few for my mother to cook. Fishing became one of my main excuses for going to the willows at the river's edge. The San Juan was a dangerous river. Its sandbanks were continually caving in. Children were occasionally thrown into the fast current by such a fall and sometimes drowned. But a riverbank was a place for a boy to love, full of polished pebbles of granite, marble, and agate.

I was busy there one afternoon when something wet nuzzled me. I looked up into the face of a sheep. Then another joined him and another, and more and more until I was nearly crowded off the bank into the river. They were part of a huge flock being herded through town by ranchers. The first sheep that nuzzled me was coal black. The others were white. In the hour and a half it took for the entire flock to pass I counted six more black ones, so I knew the flock totaled about 700. The black sheep are for counting—usually one black for every hundred white.

"Kent, what happened to your hand?" my mother asked, when she saw a big, ugly blister on it one evening. I didn't dare tell her that hot lead had spilled on me when I copied the big boys and made lead sinkers and rings at a fire behind the house. What turned out to be a good burn remedy for me that April afternoon is now standard first-aid treatment everywhere. Rushing to a nearby ditch, I plunged in my aching hand. The cold water took away the pain, so I kept dipping my hand the rest of the day.

As soon as the blister healed I resumed manufacturing lead items. But, cautious from casualty, I worked at the spring beside Navajo Twins. Nowadays, sightseers stop to admire Bluff's redstone twins . . . two human-looking columns of carved sandstone near the spring. Every time I pass I am reminded that it was the place where the big boys used to get me to fight the rest of the boys in school by offering me their orange peelings and the white pulp inside. Sometimes, as a special treat, they even gave me a bite of banana. The big boys also taught me how to make a big noise by throwing bullets into a fire, then hiding behind a tree while they exploded.

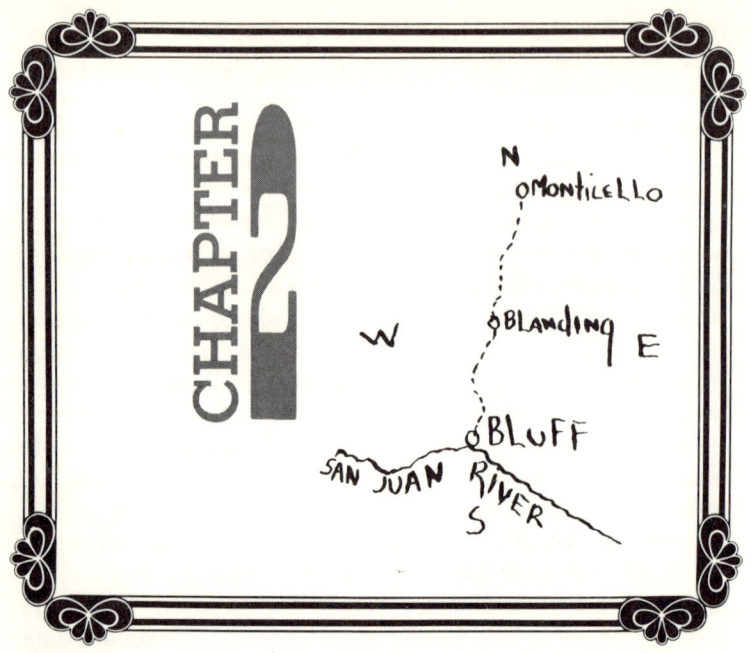

CHAPTER 2

"Hurry and pack your things, Kent," my oldest sister said to me, when I came home the last day of school. "We're moving to Monticello." I didn't know whether I liked that or not. But my father was through trapping in Monument Valley and on Navajo Mountain. He wanted to be back at his homestead at Dodge, ten miles south of Monticello. I bid my own silent good-bye to Bluff's handsome houses of native stone. Monticello up north was a small stock-raising and farming community at the foot of Blue Mountain. We settled on land called Dodge, ten miles out of town. The whole family farmed our homestead there for a year and a half, with inspiring views of the mountain to encourage us.

Clearing the homestead land at Dodge was a heavy task. One time we burned 100 acres at once. Starting and controlling such a fire was a large undertaking. We gathered straw for a week and spread it in a line that stretched out of view. One day, when the wind was just right, we lit it and let it roar. We ran all day with pitchforks of burning hay to start the fire in new places.

My brother, Alfred, and I rode together to do our work on one old, lazy horse. Lacking spurs, we hit him with a sharp stick to make him gallop.

Dad used to freight our groceries and supplies in from the railhead at Thompson. He took me several times. They were cherished camping trips. We were going after a load of apples on one of those trips. When we reached Dry Valley he handed me the reins, saying, "You drive, Kent, while I get us a fine supper." He got down with his .22 rifle and walked alongside as I proudly drove the team of four horses. Each time he stopped to shoot he got a rabbit. We had a feast that night when we camped. On the return trip he hunted successfully again. This time we raided our new supplies for apples to stew with our rabbits. I still remember how good it all tasted.

For contrast, the following winter my Uncle Mons invited me along when he hauled our wheat to town by sleigh. The strong north wind blew against me until I was too stiff to move. "Come on, Kent," he said, "get out and walk." He managed to warm me up a bit that way. Several times he tied our large shovel behind the sleigh. I was small enough to stand on it and ride along behind. Back at Dodge I helped Alf try the shovel ride, but he was too big for it.

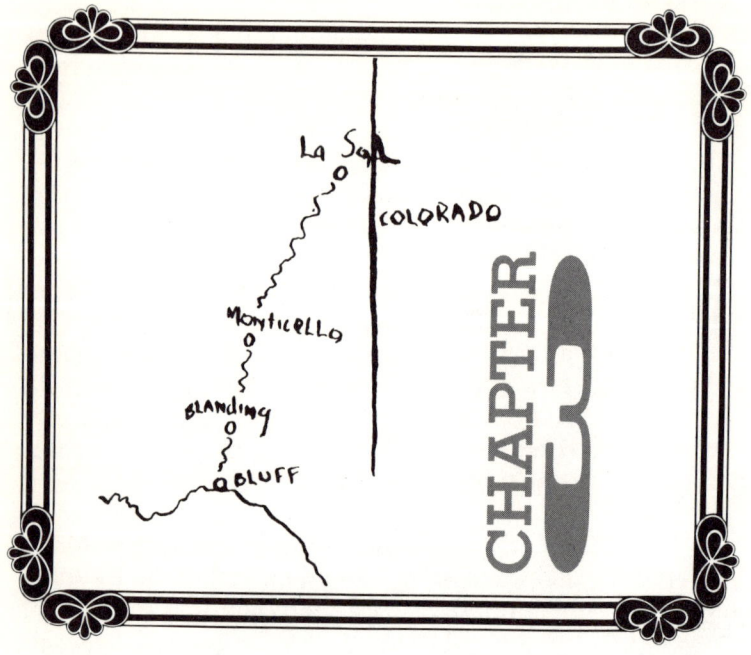

CHAPTER 3

When my father was offered a job as foreman of a ranch at La Sal, 40 miles farther north, he moved the family up there. He needed the cash the salary would give him. Everything we owned was piled into two great wagons. Dad drove one. My Uncle Mons drove the other. Alf and I each climbed on top of a load. We rode like kings all day, monarchs of moving, to the home Dad had already chosen for us. Mons returned a few days later to Dodge to continue living and farming there.

Our ranch at La Sal was a pretty place at the foot of the east slope of those beautiful La Sal Mountains you can see from Highway 163. La Sal was a ranching community with about twenty houses clustered around a store and post office, and ten more homes within ten miles.

I always think about my boyhood at La Sal as one of the nicest parts of my life. We had a lot of fun. We were five miles from the post office and store, and the good part of it was that we were ten miles from the school.

The ranch of my boyhood days at La Sal—one of the nicest parts of my life.

The first winter, there were not enough students for the La Sal school to open at all. My parents had to send Willie, our oldest sister, to Grandpa and Grandma Smith in Salt Lake City for school. The rest of us had lessons at home with Mother.

My brothers and I would spend the winter trapping bobcats, coyotes, and skunks. We got pretty good at it. Dad taught us. He was a good trapper. Alf found a rusty old bear trap. He worked on it all winter and turned it back into a good one. He gave it to me. I still have it but I have never caught anything in it.

The cowboys left their horses at our ranch, and we gentled them. Every day found us touring the country by horse, exploring, and setting traps. On several occasions, it was my job to ride a horse over the forty miles from La Sal to Monticello to deliver the animal to my Uncle Mons. Transportation back was my responsibility. I always managed to pick up a highway ride.

Some Paiutes came riding by one day and camped near us for a month. They had fine pitch baskets hanging from their saddles to carry water. They got jobs cutting brush, and I used to visit them. They were pretty with their bright and colorful clothes.

Each spring, there were several herds of sheep in the area. The first time we rode out to a sheep camp, we found Joe Turk holding a bleating lamb.

"Look here, boys," he called. He dipped his fingers in a pan of milk, then put them in the lamb's mouth. The lamb started to suck. Joe did it over and over. Then, he held his fingers in the milk, and the lamb sucked his fingers again, this time in the pan. After several trials, the lamb got the idea. Soon, he was drinking naturally from the pan.

"Why go to all that trouble, Joe?" I asked. "Can't his mother feed him?"

"This here's a dogie lamb. His mother won't claim him. You boys take home the rest of the dogies, teach them to drink, and raise them through the summer. The ranch owner will buy them back from you in the fall." After that, we raised up to 30 dogies a season and made a few dollars selling them back.

Even though he was nice to us, I was afraid of Joe Turk. He had great whiskers, trimmed to stick out fiercely from his face, and two terrifying lumps on his head, a large and a small one. I asked another cowboy, Bull Montana, "Why does Joe Turk have those two lumps on his head?"

"Well, Kent," Bull said, confidentially, "he was in a fight with some outlaws at Robbers' Roost. He got hit on the head with a club that had two knots, one big and one little." For years after that, I studied Joe Turk's lumps, whenever I saw him, to determine the size of the knots on the stick.

It was always my job to run the cows out of the pasture before we milked them. It was a big operation to milk up to ten head a day by hand. I liked to go barefoot, starting with the early days of Spring. Not all the early days were warm. The morning frost on the pasture grass almost froze my feet. As a result, I watched the cows carefully. When one dropped a steaming green cowpie, I would run over and stand in it. "Eeeeeeh," I breathed. I surely enjoyed the warmth. Just before we reached the barn gate, where a creek came through, I washed my feet on the way back—but not a bit more than I had to in that ice cold water.

I didn't know I had an audience one morning, until a man's laughter made me look up from the creek. The man on horseback said, "Got your own heating system, eh, sonny?" He bent to one side of his horse and tugged at a strap and buckle. Then, with a quick half-turn in his seat, he put a hand on each end of his saddle, lifted himself free, and landed on the ground . . . on one leg. He untied his lariat to release a set of crutches I had not noticed. I had never seen him before, but I knew who he was. Lee Larson was famous in our area as the one-legged cowboy. As I stood amazed at his performance, he added, "Glad you washed 'em off," then swung briskly away on his crutches to see Dad.

Lee could do everything the other cowboys did, camping out for weeks at a time with his pack horse while tending his cattle over in Greasewood Silvey's Pocket and East Coyote Country. He did his own farm work, too, mowing, raking hay, hauling it, and anything else the ranch operation demanded. Later, when we boys got to know him, we often stayed overnight at his house after fishing the creek. His wife made us welcome.

When Lee Larson got married and brought his bride to his La Sal Creek home, my sister, Willie, and her friend, Lora Douglass, were so eager to meet her that they rode for two hours to get there and ask for a glass of water. They went away with their water and a mighty fine impression of the young Mrs. Larson.

I was about 7½ the day I fell from a horse in front of their door. Mrs. Larson ran out and held me in her arms. With a great shove, I pushed her and squirmed to the ground.

"I don't want any old lady picking me up," I howled.

On another day, I was standing beside Lee Larson, watching flood water rage down La Sal Creek, when the wind blew his new Stetson into it. He felt so bad about losing that new hat that I walked for a mile or more along the creek, hunting for it, hoping it would get caught in the driftwood so that I could find it for him. It would have been in good shape if I had. Those Stetsons were strong hats. The cowboy choice was grey or black, and they all wore them big, high, and rounded. . . . No plowshares crease in *their* crowns.

On my way home from one of those visits at the Larsons, I was just coming through the gate when I heard my father shouting.

"Get out! Get out and go home and don't come back!" Astonishing words to hear from a usually gentle man. Past me shuffled deaf Dilly Crouse, with his one leg shorter than the other, muttering what sounded like threats.

"What happened, Dad?" I ran to ask.

"That obnoxious old character," he answered. "He's been here arguing with me about everything all day. Now he says he's going to kill the foreman of the road crew, because he says he didn't get his pay." Dilly was a rough character. Everyone knew he always carried a small automatic pistol in a shoulder holster inside his coat. He was a sure shot with it, too. He used to shoot rabbits in the head with a quick draw, one bullet per rabbit, for his meals. The cowboys' style was different: they carried carbines in their saddle scabbards. Lee Larson carried a 30-30 carbine in his.

Of course, I asked Joe Wilson if he thought Dilly would kill the foreman. Joe Wilson was my cowboy hero. He came regularly to irrigate the alfalfa fields. Joe had been through a real Indian battle when just a kid. Once when Joe and his brother were herding cattle a few miles out of Moab, they were ambushed by Utes. The Utes shot Joe in the ankle. He fell off his horse. The Indians fired a shot to finish him. The bullet cut off the bridge of his nose and put out one eye. They left him for dead, but an Indian woman on horseback picked him up and carried him to the edge of Moab, where she deposited him and motioned to the whites that he was there. He survived with a little round stump for a nose and only one eye. His ankle never healed properly, so he had to build up the shoe for that foot on the outside by putting the sole on its side instead of flat. Joe carried a 44-40 carbine. It didn't shoot as far as other guns.

When Joe Wilson came to irrigate, I stopped everything else and followed him all day. He taught me how to catch prairie dogs. Uncle Charlie Redd paid ten cents apiece for their tails. Joe would pour water in their holes and catch their heads with a shovel when they came up, which killed them and prevented their biting or escaping. We cut off and pocketed their tails; then we threw the bodies back in the holes and covered them up. I was sure good at drowning out prairie dogs when old Joe was helping me.

Back home, we strung up the tails on lines and dried them. When we took them to Uncle Charlie, he came out in front of his general store and counted the tails and paid us. The first time I followed Joe, I saw him take out a dark brown square, bite off a piece, and put it in his mouth.

"What's that, Joe?"

"It's chewin' tobaccy. Want to try some?"

"Sure," I said, full of importance. He broke off a small chunk, handed it to me, and said,

"Be careful and don't swaller it."

How it burned. But Joe was watching me, so I kept it in my mouth. I began to feel sick. Then Joe spat, wonderfully far. So that's how you got rid of it! I spat. Every day that Joe Wilson was around, he would give me my own little hunk of tobacco. I would put it in my shirt pocket just the way he kept his, then break off a tiny piece, chew, and spit. There was something very special about Joe's technique that I thought accounted for our success. When the animals' bodies were pushed back into their holes, a squirt of Joe's tobacco juice sailed in, too. With steady practice, I could spit about half as far as old Joe could, as we went along, drowning prairie dogs. We were real good buddies.

"Come on, Alf," I said to my older brother. "Let's go climb Mt. Peale, the one the cowboys talk about." We asked our folks.

"It's a long way to go in a day," Mother said.

"We can camp overnight in that empty cowboy cabin at the mountain," said Alfred who was 11.

"Yes," said Dad. "I'll give you a team of horses to hitch to the old, two-wheeled cart."

"Take me, too," pleaded Melvin, our younger brother, who was 6.

"All right," I agreed. I was 8.

"Don't let those horses get away from you when you unhitch them," cautioned our parents, as we started out on the Fourth of July. "They'll come right home without you." So we hauled some hay and grain to leave with the horses to keep them from running away.

We were off to climb that mountain. We were a little scared. We wondered how steep it would be. It was going to be our first experience camping out in the country by ourselves. Melvin kept rattling a piece of chain that was his special treasure at the moment.

"Are you going to carry that chain to the top of the mountain?" I asked him, when we reached the cabin for the night.

"No," he said, solemnly. "I'm going to bury it." He and I always had secret caches around in the hills in which we hid our treasures. I'll bet that today I could go back and find that chain.

Even though we started up before sunrise the next morning, it was a big, long, hard day's climb. "I'm awfully hot and thirsty," Melvin said, as we struggled up the sliderock that rolled out from under our feet. Joe Wilson had lent us his 44-40 carbine to protect us from bears. There were many black bears that stood five feet tall on their hind feet.

"Do you think we'll meet a bear?" asked Melvin.

"Pretty good chance," said Alf. "John Rohwer shot one at Spring Canyon last week." Spring Canyon was two or three miles from the ranch.

"Did you see the skin, Alf? I was home when he came by with it, to show Dad."

"I missed it then, but I met him a week later riding to the Deer Creek pasture. It was still spread over his saddle." We took turns carrying Joe's carbine, but we were grateful that Alf was big enough, strong enough, and willing enough to carry it most of the time. When we got past the timberline, Alf set it down a moment.

"I hear water," he said. We stopped to listen. There was the sound of water pouring somewhere underneath us on the dry sliderock. Was there an underground spring so close to the summit? Melvin looked eager. We took a few steps and found patches of snow. Three dusty little faces sucked some of that nice, wet July present. We concluded that melting snow was the stream we could hear under the sliderock. A small animal, as furry as a chinchilla, had been eating the snow. It did not run away, but stayed to look at us. Another appeared. Before our climb was over, we saw several of them, all quite tame. Those tiny creatures, probably coneys, must have lived on the scanty grass growing up there between the rocks.

Just a short climb farther was the top. It astonished me. The day was unusually clear. I had never before seen so much of the land. South, I could see plainly Blue Mountain at Monticello. North, all the way to the Book Cliffs, were pink and yellow and red canyons and mesas. To the east, I could see Lone Cone Mountain and the San Juan range in Colorado. The Henry Mountains showed up like shadows far away against the western horizon, but between them and me were all kinds of colors and shapes of land. A dark line cut through in places. That dark line was the great canyon of the Colorado River. We all stood silent.

"How big," I thought. "I'm going to get into all those places some day." I guess that was the first time I was aware of all the color in the land of my home. The clouds seemed extra white and the sky a deeper blue than I had ever noticed before.

We were tired as all heck. No one had told us that a mountain like Peale that's over 12,000 feet is a tall one. Even though we rested at the top, our knees kept buckling on the way down so that we tripped often. Yet we got to the bottom and home that night, bursting to tell our folks about our big adventure. They were retelling it for years. The cowboys seemed impressed. It pleased me to hear Joe Wilson say, "What! You three boys got to the top of Mt. Peale?"

That was the summer the Taylors from California spent three weeks with us. They had no children and took a great liking to Alf.

"Let Alfred come to live with us this winter in California," they begged our parents. "He can attend school there." The school advantage could always persuade our parents. Alf went off for the winter of '25 and went back to California again for the winter '26. I felt lucky they were fonder of Alf than of me. I would not have cared to leave La Sal for school anywhere.

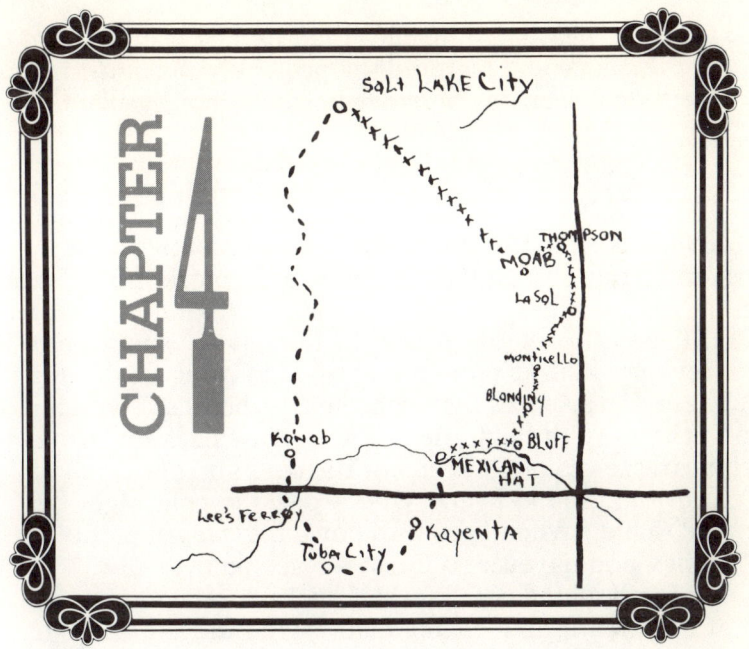

CHAPTER 4

After four years at La Sal, we were moving back again to the Dodge homestead near Monticello where the population had grown to 500. I think my mother was secretly glad to get us out of what she considered poor company—out of the bunkhouse, where I could always be found listening to the cowboys—and back to the Boy Scouts and Sunday School of Monticello. I knew I'd miss my cowboy friends and their tales. Joe Wilson took me to see Jail Rock before I had to say good-bye.

"John Jackson had his cattle here," Joe said, "and his wife was helping tend them. They ran out of food and supplies, so John says to her, 'Honey, I'll put you down in this big, deep pit in the rock. Then the wild cowboys around Dry Valley will not be able to find you while I'm gone all the way to Moab after supplies.' So he let her down into the pit with a rope and a canteen of water and whatever bit of supplies they had left. But when he got to Moab, he got drunk with the other cowboys and stayed four days. When he came back, his wife was almost starved to death and madder than hell." I peered down over the edge and pictured the poor woman sputtering. She didn't seem a bit smarter than her husband to me.

When school opened in Monticello, my father bought an old house in town: four walls and a roof, with 2 X 4's standing up throughout the interior to mark the different rooms. When we retired to our bedrooms we could still see all over the house. In the center was a large fireplace, and at one end, a wood-burning cookstove. There were spaces between the floorboards. The wind whistled up through them. Even straw pads under our mattresses couldn't keep out the cold air that came up from the ground below. One especially cold night Alf said to me, "When I grow up I'm going to earn plenty of money and have the tightest house you ever saw."

It was an all-day job for Alf and me to take the team of horses and the wagon about seven miles outside of town every Saturday, to hunt for juniper and piñon wood to burn in the fireplace and cookstove. We had to drag 300-pound logs with the team and lift them up ourselves on the wagon. In the dark we returned with our wagonload. To this day I think it was Willie's beau who made this seem like one of the trying jobs I had to do.

"He's selfish," I stormed to Alf. "He keeps her sitting up until midnight and they use up all the wood we work so hard to get."

"He's coming tonight," said Alf. "Then, we'll have to get up early to cut more, so Mother can cook breakfast." What never occurred to us was the remarkable courtship the young man was conducting in an open-view house.

I had missed a great deal of school. It was hard catching up. A wonderful cousin helped me with my lessons. She and the other girls around me coached me in class in whispers when my answers to the teacher's questions were slow in coming. Melvin liked school. Of course, he was younger when we returned permanently to Monticello, so he had a steadier diet of it right from the start. Perhaps that's why he has become a professor.

On the way home from school one day, cowboy Tony Lester paid me fifteen cents for currying his bay mare, hitched at the barber shop on Main Street.

"If I could turn all them Indian relics from Salt Creek into cash, Kent," he said, "I'd pay you more."

"What relics? Where's Salt Creek, Tony?"

"Aw, you town folks got plenty of sights waiting for you. Salt Creek's a canyon in the Needles. It's so purty, I like to be in the rough old son-of-a-gun now. And all up and down the canyon there's caves with Indian ruins. I found some turquoise beads last month, and a pottery jar and some feathers this week."

"Is that one?" I asked, pointing to his hat.

"Yep." I know now that the bright green feather he sported was brought here by Indian trade ten centuries ago from Central America. That was the first time I ever heard about the Needles. I was to hear about them many times more, but only from the cowboys. The Needles, just twenty-five crowflight miles from Monticello, seemed more remote than Europe. I decided it was an easy name to remember for a place too hard for anyone else to reach.

For sixty years the cowboys from Moab, Monticello, and Blanding took care of their cattle summer and winter in the Needles. In those days, Cave Springs wasn't the Canyonlands park office, as it is now. It was range camp for some of the lonesomest stockmen in a lonesome country. Those cowboys of my Monticello boyhood loved to tell tales of their predecessors, the wild cowboys of the Carlisle Company . . . twice-told tales that belonged also to the town folk. The Carlisle Company, owned by two Englishmen of that name in the 1890's, ran their cattle all over the country. They hired all the floating characters who came along, many of them outside the law. Those wild ones shot up the town every time they arrived. They kept the citizens jittery with fights, thefts, and murders. Long before I was a schoolboy, however, the original company had been sold and parceled out. Its former headquarters continued to be known as the Carlisle Ranch. Today it is called Carlisle as though it were a town.

As far back as anyone knows, there was a permanent spring in Cave Springs. It must have been a favorite camping place for the ancient Indians. A thousand years ago, they left red paintings on the back wall. Imagine what a cool oasis the cave was in summer for the cowboys who had been working over those hot, dry canyons! With no change of temperature inside, the cave managed to be a warm haven when snow fell on Angel Arch and Potsy's Rock.

My father invited two stockmen for supper one night. They listened to him describe some eroded cliffs he'd gone out of his way to see in Dry Valley—where he went to purchase a portable sawmill.

"C. A.," one said, "just go in and see them spirals in the Needles. Why, there's hundreds of 'em. Every one a different shape. All in different colors."

"It's a pretty country, but it's rough," said another.

"How are the trails there, Les?" I heard my father ask Les Young one morning in front of our flour mill.

"C. A.," he answered, "they're so bad, half the time I think the horse won't make it and I'll lose my supplies. Rest of the time, I'm afraid he'll get there and I'll be stuck with your flour for my sourdough after all." My father laughed, but he knew what slickrock and narrow ledges meant. He had been hired as part of the first government surveying team over Elk Mountain.

Those cowboys were always talking about how pretty the spires were and how bad the trails were in the Needles. But it was John Rohwer who fired my imagination about the Needles.

I listened while he told my father about a cache he had found on Dark Canyon Mesa. It was a safe made of rocks. Could it have contained some of the outlaws' gold? He had not had the tools or time to uncover it then, and although he went back over and over again (actually, until he was an old man), he never could relocate it. The floods must have washed sand over it. He went on to describe some Indian ruins he found in the Needles.

"Skeletons so long," he said, "they must have been giants." I could see that my dad wanted to go there and see them as much as I did.

"It would be nice to explore over there. When we get caught up in our work, we might go and look around."

"Let's do it, Dad." The day we were "caught up" never came. Years later I took him in on a Jeep trip. We had all had to work too hard on the homestead to have time to explore. But a decade later I went after Rohwer's cache on Dark Canyon Mesa. I hadn't forgotten. I've never found it . . . yet.

The night Rohwer told his story I was polishing part of a gun after supper while the grown folks talked. I wasn't allowed to have a gun. Of course I wanted one, so I would get a part here and there and somewhere else and hide them under the woodpile. No one knew what I was preparing when I polished a piece at a time. When I had enough parts, I built my own gun.

Chester Black, who ran the Monticello flour mill, was my authority on guns. We had many a serious gun discussion. We would begin with the latest models, while he weighed in a truck of grain and checked a sample. He adjusted the wheat spouts pouring into the bins. Then he drew out and watered the next day's supply for grinding as we switched to gun stocks. Following him up the narrow wood stairs, I debated gun barrels with him. I would peer into the glass viewers on the second floor as he did to watch the first sifting of bran and flour slide by, but our remarks were concerned with gun loading devices. Sometimes he would dip into the flour stalls to check the refinement. Then he would raise his arms, floury to the elbows, to demonstrate the best way of aligning sights.

Downstairs again, on a December afternoon, I was hooking printed bags on the loader, one at a time, as he filled them. I had just removed one and was running the top through the sewing machine when he asked, "Kent, when is your birthday?"

"Next month."

"Well, I want to be the first to give you a birthday present." He drew from a cabinet full of weevil sprays and brooms a rifle so long that when I held the marvel in my hands it was as tall as I was. It was a 45-70 Springfield, Model 1873.

Fortunately, a truck pulled up just then for weighing so that I didn't have to try to say anything to Chester for a while. I could not have spoken.

Just a few weeks later I shot my first deer with it. After years of constant use, when it no longer seemed sacrilegious to alter it, I shortened the stock and cut off the end of the barrel so that the rifle would fit me better. I still have it among my prized possessions, but not as a museum piece. It is still a fine, serviceable gun.

In 1927 my folks purchased a new Dodge touring car, the open style that chilled back seat passengers—of which I was generally one. What destination could be far enough for such a splendid vehicle? The end of the world. They planned a trip to Salt Lake City and took me and our hired man, Alex Jameson. Some scenes still stand out. As we crossed the Green River, Alex said, "There's a coyote. Wait a minute, till I get my pistol out. I'll shoot him."

We stopped. Alex unpacked his trunk. No gun. The coyote waited curiously. Then Alex unpacked his suitcase. The gun was there. The coyote waited patiently. Alex loaded the gun. The coyote stood obligingly at the side of the road. At last Alex fired and missed. Only then the coyote ran.

My grandparents Smith gave us an old washing machine when our visit with them in Salt Lake City ended. It was no problem to load it in the car, just a matter of pushing me a little farther into the car's wall. We drove south to visit more Frost relatives in Kanab, Utah. When we left them, they warned, "Watch out for Mr. Moon. When he's angry, you can hear him swear from across the river." Mr. Moon was the operator of Lee's Ferry, and that's where we were headed. Sure enough, we knew when we had arrived. We could hear him from the other side. He was swearing some cars off his ferry as we drove up. Their drivers had been hesitant to go off into the mud along the river bank. He swore at them as —naturally—they got stuck in it. Then he swore worst of all as he hauled them out with a team of horses.

I worried. We would surely be stuck, and he would swear at us. My hands gripped the seat. My eyes pleaded with Mr. Moon to be kind. Alf was disappointed later back home when I told him we had made it without trouble. He thought it would have been fun to hear how bad the swearing could be.

The rest of our route took us through the reservation. I saw Navajos tending herds of sheep and goats. I saw hogans. I saw the strange rock shapes of Monument Valley. Our dirt road was rough. Once I thought the washing machine would land on top of me.

A vast circle was completed, as we ended by going through Mexican Hat and Bluff. Then on through Blanding . . . and back to Monticello. Around the world for a ten-year-old boy. It was nice to revisit Bluff. On our stop there my father pointed out to me how important Bluff had been in the old days, at the edge of the Navajo reservation and close to Four Corners (where four states meet). The early settlers had moved in to make peace with the Indians and stem the stream of outlaws from three adjacent states (plus enough from Texas to make the settlers think that state was next door, too). For men in trouble it was convenient to be where crossing a state line meant safety from the law. Bluff pioneers had their hands full, maintaining order while wresting a living from the land.

Back at Dodge for the summer, I found the swimming hole that every boy has to have. Did many go so far for theirs? Dodge, our homestead, was on a mesa that jutted into Montezuma Canyon, 2,000 feet below. It was a rough hike down through sage and oak brush, juniper and piñon woods, and sliding talus slopes to the delightful pool where water poured over a six-foot waterfall. On each return I took a different hard climb, to learn more about the country—up through serviceberry, cactus, and flaming Indian paintbrush.

I could have ridden a horse, but I preferred hiking. I would walk the ten miles into Monticello and back rather than catch an unwilling horse. Most of ours were unwilling. My uncle had started the line with a race horse. All her descendants were the world's orneriest. Any missing wild traits in them were added when my father bought forty head of wild horses from Lee Larson. The menfolk had to bring them all the way from Island Mesa at the Colorado border, tied two together.

We ended up with a lot of crazy horses. They scared easily, would not cross bridges, and often took off when hitched to a wagon.

I remember several thrilling rides with my father on the wagon when the horses started running away. I would just sit there and hang on, while he tried to get them under control. It was exciting, too, when my father and Uncle Mons would hook up some colts to break them to the harness and wagon.

"Come along, Kent," they might say if I were there. I would jump in eagerly for a wild ride as the young horses went tearing out through the field as though they would never come back. Our dry farming required so much riding that I must have tried every horse, and I never liked any of them. Alf always liked horses. I think this is one of his joys as a farmer today. But my experiences conditioned me against them.

Once a week it was Alf's job and mine to hitch up the team to the family wagon and go five miles up Verdure Canyon for several barrels of water for household use. We dipped it out of the creek with buckets and filled barrels. That's doing it the hard way. We tied canvas on top of each barrel so the water wouldn't splash out on the way home.

Not all my troubles were with horses. My father and uncle bought a large Holstein bull, very mean, that had a habit of getting infuriated when he saw a man riding a horse. His nose was out of shape because he had managed to tear the ring out of it. One day the bull attacked Alf's horse and knocked it down.

Oddly enough, I was able to drive the bull around on foot. When I threw rocks at him he would run along with the cows. But one day he just stood there, bellowing and pawing the dirt. I picked up two large stones and was getting close enough to throw them when his eyes rolled around until I could see the whites. I knew something was going to happen. I threw one stone, hit him on the head, and started running for the fence.

The bull caught up with me just as I was ready to crawl through. He knocked me down inside the fence and butted me several times before pushing me underneath the wire. I thought he would try to tear the fence down to come after me, and I was too bruised to run. Instead he went off peacefully to join the cows, while I cried. My brother, Melvin, came up leading my horse. I was beginning to mount, when along came Uncle Wilford. He could see that I had been crying.

"Kent, you're all covered with dust. What's the matter?"

"The bull butted me through the fence."

"I will get my gun and kill the bull!" he said.

"Oh, no, you don't need to do that," I sobbed. "I'll keep out of the bull's way next time." I kept my word.

"Friend of the hermits" I must have been. Alf marveled at the number of pals I had in remote corners of nearby canyons. His close friends were always from town—boys his age from school or farming. On my hikes to the bottom of beautiful Montezuma Canyon, I discovered Joe Duckett. He was homesteading. A remarkably self-sufficient, solitary man: rarely going to town, he raised alfalfa, corn, peaches, and cows. He ground his corn into flour and dried his peaches for his winter fruit supply. His dugout house, with a canvas top, had a 16" plank bench running its length past the fireplace. The bench was table, chair, and bed for him. His home was a tiny compartment. Through the years, the canvas top kept wearing out at the ends, where the water dripped off, forcing Joe to keep moving the bench towards the fireplace. I thought this was the reason he was so exceedingly stoop-shouldered—he had to lean forward to avoid touching his roof while sitting in his house.

Joe Duckett became a homesteader but had come into the country as a prospector. In 1935, somebody was riding up the canyon past Duckett's home and noted that Joe had apparently not been around for several days. He organized a search and found Joe a mile from his cabin, dead in the bottom of a wash. His horse must have rolled on top of him in a fall from the trail. His body, badly decomposed, was buried near his tiny dugout in the canyon he loved so well.

The early miners, like Duckett, did things the hard way, drilling their holes with hand steel and hammer in the rock face. Only the excitement of gold could have lured men into such hard toil. Blue Mountain was buzzing with it. The Gold Queen Mine and the Dream Mine were firing men's ambitions and eating up their capital.

Legends persist. Three that I know converge on one area. It makes me feel there is some truth in them. Men like Joe Duckett and Old Man West worked modestly. West retired from mining engineering to live as a hermit on Blue Mountain. I used to go up on my skis to visit him in his cabin overnight. It took all day to ski up the eight miles. I could come back in two hours.

Old Man West was starving to death. But he was a proud old guy. He used to scavenge the dump heaps of other cabins and bring back the best-looking cans. They were lined up on his shelves, and he would say, "See all the supplies I've got." I once went around and tapped the cans when he went out. Almost every one sounded empty. He used to read old magazines and got to believing he was an associate of the authors. He would report the latest stories as though the authors had given him private previews.

Early one spring he talked me into going with him around the south end of Blue Mountain to put claims on several of the old gold mines there. The snow got deeper as we hiked with packs on our backs. We kept breaking through the crust and falling in up to our hips. We reached a cabin at Cold Spring; its windows were out, but it had a fireplace. We got the fire going, cooked our dinner, and arranged a bed by turning a table upside down. Even with a blanket under each of us and one over, I'm sure we might have frozen had it not been for my dog. He slept on our feet and kept them warm.

The next day the wind was blowing so hard we could not progress farther up the mountain, so we did the only reasonable thing: turned around and came down, giving up our prospecting venture.

Jim Hicks, blind in one eye, was another Montezuma Canyon hermit I liked. I used to stop and see him often. He had an old cylinder-type phonograph which he cranked up by hand and played for me. He always had skunk scent around his place. It seemed that he was in a permanent battle with the skunks. One day when I came by, the smell of skunks was unusually strong—even for Hicks' home.

"Well, Mr. Hicks," I said, "it smells as though you have been fighting with the skunks again."

"Yes," he said, "those damn skunks get underneath my cabin all the time, and I have to trap them. Young feller, don't let a skunk squirt scent in your eye. It will make you go blind. That is why I can't see out of one eye very good right now. The skunk squirted in my eye."

Now my family's experience is the opposite. Alf was fitted for eyeglasses. He hated them. "I'm not going to wear them," he told me. He buried them out in a field. Next day a skunk, trapped in our storehouse, fired at unsuspecting Alf and hit his eyes. Yelling with pain, Alf ran to Mother, who was in the kitchen washing dishes. When she learned what had happened, she grabbed the dishwater as the handiest thing and rinsed his eyes with all of it. By the next morning Alf's eyes felt better. His sight was fine. In fact, he never wore glasses again in his life. So his opinion of the effect of skunk spray on eyes is different from Jim Hicks'. Or perhaps you have to have dishwater handy to offset it.

I still relish the picture of my first overnight hiking trip. My friend, Elmo Red, and I decided to go down Montezuma Canyon for our Easter vacation. It was the prettiest place we knew, with its smooth, bulging redrock walls, and cliffs dotted with green. Indian caves and campsites aplenty were to be found there.

"We need packs, Kent," said Elmo. We looked around and found some gunny sacks lying in a corner.

"Try this on, Elmo," I said, cutting slits in one for armholes. "Couldn't be better. We have packs." I wonder why we needed packs. Beyond putting in a blanket apiece, I can recall only a two-quart bottle of home-canned cherries which we carried all day and ate for dinner that night. We made camp at the spot where Verdure Creek runs into Montezuma. It was a long, cold night, because we knew so little about organizing campfires. We didn't stock enough wood. What we did gather was the fast-burning variety. When it got late and dark our wood supply was gone, and we remained awake most of the night, pulling up sagebrush around our camp to keep the fire going. Morning dawned on a couple of tired boys.

We stopped at Joe Duckett's to talk to him. Two miles farther on was a large cave about a hundred feet up the slickrock, with Moqui steps leading to it. I managed to climb up into the cave, but it wasn't easy. Then I was afraid to come down. I sat there about half an hour, studying the steps and deciding just where to put my feet and hands on the way down. Elmo looked so secure there on the solid ground. I was surely happy when I finally joined him.

We found some wild parsnips on the way home to ease the hunger that was beginning to attack us. It was an instructive trip. No one starts out as an expert.

I became rich. $500 in cash came to me during my last year of school. Our principal, who was a good ice skater, planned a skating party at the reservoir for the upper classmen. A boy who could not swim fell through thin ice in the center. A teacher and I went to his aid. Both of us fell in. With a small knife I had on my belt, I stabbed into solid ice and pulled myself out. Then, stabbing farther into the ice, I extended my feet to the teacher. He used his hold on my feet, first to lift out the boy, then himself, while I hung on to my knife. Another teacher recommended us for the Carnegie Award. The teacher and I, who had never anticipated such a thing, received medals and cash awards.

I sat reading my check over and over. "I'll buy a motorcycle," I told my folks. But they had other ideas. Alf was on their side. He thought the best thing a person could do was invest in land. My sisters put their weight into it on my parents' side, too. Only Melvin stood listening, too young to have his say. After more than one family council they persuaded me to use my $500 as a down payment on some land at Dodge near the homestead. It has now become one of the best farms in San Juan County. Its wheat production paid for the land many years ago.

CHAPTER 6

At my father's request, we used our portable sawmill to cut some of the ponderosa pine in a side canyon. This led to hauling the sawmill around to neighboring farms to saw their pines. A few months later, we set up the mill in our Monticello yard. When I was 16 and Alf was 18, we loaded the sawmill on an iron-wheeled wagon behind our tractor and pulled it down through Blanding and out into Johnson's Creek. It was a rough road. Alf reached for the two-quart jar of milk to start our camp supper going.

"It won't pour," he said. Then he looked in. "How about that? There's a big ball of butter in the mouth of the jar."

I mused, "Next time those cowboys tell us about the rough trails in the Needles. . . ."

In various new sites on Blue Mountain we operated our sawmill for years. Uncle Mons dragged in logs with a team of horses. Alf and two men and I ran the carriage that cut the logs into lumber. The hardest job was carrying away the lumber and slabs. Some of the 2 X 6's weighed 150 pounds each. My back still aches when I think about picking up those slabs. In my spare moments between carrying, I would have to run around into the sawdust pit and remove the sawdust with a large scoop shovel. That was hard work.

John Rohwer continued to show up from time to time and regale my father with his tales. He turned to me one evening before leaving and said, "How would you like to go coyote hunting with me tomorrow, Kent?" He had never paid any attention to me before. I was flattered. We went up in the mountain, looking for coyote dens. He showed me how to follow their tracks to the den—which is always a hole in the ground or a cubbyhole far back in the rocks. It takes work to dig them out. I brought two puppies home for pets. One puppy killed some chickens. My parents put an end to him quickly. The other one grew up playing with our family dog.

In the fall I moved back to the mountain sawmill with the dog and the coyote. The coyote got wilder every day. At last he would not even come up for a piece of meat held in the hand. He did continue to go hunting with me, but when I moved back to town he would not return with me, and I never saw him again.

My hiking ability developed during those Blue Mountain days. If I had half a day I could reach the 11,500 foot peak of Blue Mountain from Monticello. The distance may be seven air miles—straight up—but it is much greater following along ledges and across canyons, through the oak brush, on foot. That mountain just drew me to it all the time.

At the end of one March day the whole family decided to drive down to see the Indian dances south of Bluff. They picked me up as I was finishing my work; there was no time for dinner. When we arrived the Indian women were preparing food for themselves and sold me two goat's meat sandwiches. I was so hungry that I finished them before joining a Bear Dance. We returned to Monticello at midnight. I asked to be let out at the edge of town.

"Where are you going?" my father asked.

"I think I'll go climb Blue Mountain," I said, already on my way. I trudged for about eight miles, through deep drifts of wet snow. As it grew later and I climbed higher, I reached frozen snow and walked on top of it. The higher I got, the harder the wind blew. The sun was just rising as I reached the summit. Every muscle in my body thrilled to the wild and mysterious feeling that comes only to one who can get into the wildest places, farthest from other people.

I had to descend as fast as I could to get out of the deep snow before it thawed. By midmorning, I had reached Blanding. It must have been a record: I had hiked about 35 miles and climbed 4,500 feet to the peak in ten hours.

My dad thought that was pretty good. "Perhaps you got extra strength from the goat meat, Kent." He used to tell people about this feat and then about my first hike.

"While we were on the homestead at Dodge Point and Kent was four years old," he would start, "I was off in Stevens Field, a mile from our house. Kent wanted to find his dad, so he went down the road, across the fields. I came back on a different road from the one he took. My wife said, 'Where's Kent?' 'I haven't seen Kent.' She said, 'Kent went to find you at Stevens Field.' I went back there. His tiny tracks showed plainly in the soft dust, and I found him a mile away, lying asleep under a bush."

The sawmill continued for years. We didn't view it as dangerous—it was merely a hard way to earn a living in a hard land. Very little of the lumber was sold for real money. It was mainly traded. Then one day the saw caught my father's hand and cut off half of it, including three fingers. Alf and I were not there. The mill crew didn't seem to know what to do, but they got him to Monticello in a wagon. A schoolteacher who understood first aid stopped the bleeding and saved his life. When he was brought by auto to the nearest hospital in Moab, another half a day away, he had good care. By the time he recovered and came home, we had dismantled the sawmill. It seemed pleasanter to concentrate on raising wheat and beans.

We heard the flour mill in town was for sale. We all

agreed that, raising as much wheat as we did, we might be able to show a profit if we owned the mill. So we were pleased the day my father announced, "I bought it." He was a man of many enterprises.

People say now he was foresighted, but there was a time when his neighbors were sure he would end in financial ruin.

While others around him were losing their land during the Depression, he stalwartly refused to give his up. He struggled desperately to clear his homestead of debt. When he emerged owning it free and clear, his credit was elevated to such local respect that he could borrow for any new venture. He invested in a new truck or tractor or mill, as need dictated. His neighbors shook their heads, but he was convinced we could work better with better equipment, whether work meant farming or some other activity.

Several other men in the county bought new tractors the year we did. They all returned them to the implement companies; it was too great an effort to meet the payments. We did custom plowing with ours, and made payments with our own wheat (which we were not allowed to store until higher winter prices, but had to turn in at harvest time's low prices). Nevertheless, after several years' hard work, the tractor was paid for. It was a 15-30 International with iron lugs on steel wheels. We used it on a job at the Colorado state line, pulling out trees to clear for a highway. It pulled so hard that all the wheel spokes got slightly bent.

It was a highly prized tool. Early one spring it broke down. Since our folks encouraged us to be independent, they had left Alf and me alone on the dry farm with all the responsibility for its operation. So we started taking the precious tractor apart. Parts were lying over the field, when our parents came out to see how we were getting along. They were dismayed at the condition of our valuable tractor.

My mother used to tell us how, on the way home, she said to Dad, "Do you think those kids will ever get that tractor together again?" He said he thought we would.

Two days later they came out and the tractor was running smoothly across the fields.

"Buy land," my father urged, and found everyone calling him a "land hog" when he followed his own advice. His belief in owning land was unswerving. He strained himself to acquire more acreage, to own it unmortgaged, and to remove the liens for mineral rights.

My grandfather had brought him here from New Mexico in 1906. They came to make brick for the Mormon church. That old brick was beautiful . . . a mellow red, because it was baked from red clay soil. When they had manufactured enough brick for the original church (built on the site of the present one) they stayed to make brick for everyone and started homesteading.

Delivering flour by truck to Monument Valley on the Reservation.

CHAPTER 7

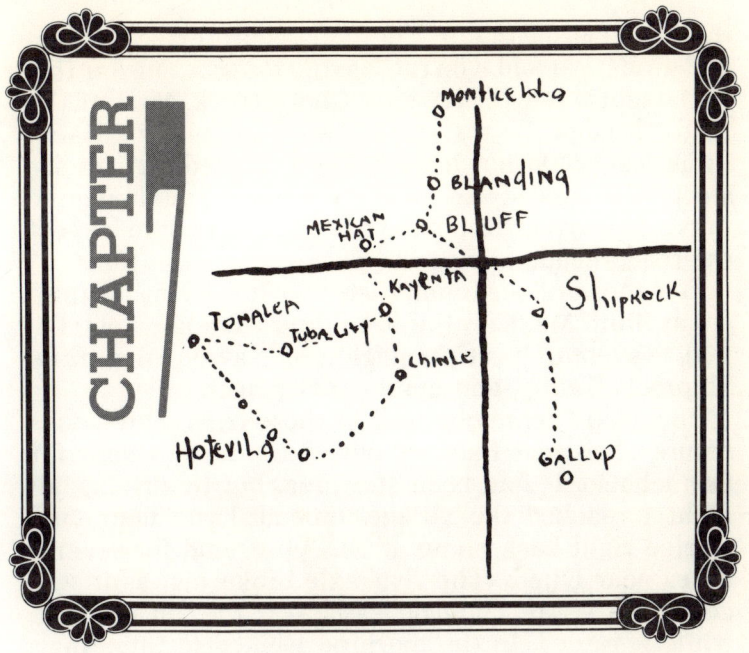

The flour mill prospered with the same kind of hard work that we had put into the sawmill. Its original one-cylinder diesel engine powered it until 1964 in Monticello. The engine stood fifteen feet high. The fly wheel weighed about 10,000 pounds. Black crude oil was a good fuel. Every three months I made a 300-mile trip down into New Mexico to get 20 barrels. Driving the truck meant that I also hauled the wheat in from storage at the local ranches and farms. I could load five tons of wheat from the ground into the truck with my big shovel in an hour and fifteen minutes.

"Kent," said Mons, when I finished loading his grain, "let me weigh a shovel full of that wheat." He was dragging just a bit when he carried it back from his scale in the barn.

"It weighs 25 pounds," he sighed.

Our flour mill products were first- and second-grade flour and bran. An interesting thing about that second-grade flour is that it makes better-flavored bread than the higher-priced flour. The Indians preferred the second-grade. We sold it on the Navajo reservation. For this we bought a new heavy-duty Chevy truck. Most of the roads through the reservation were so tough that anything less could not have made it. Rutted dirt tracks, steep hills, sand stretches in the washes, and sand dune flats ... I learned to stop the truck and get out to inspect the road ahead.

Five tons of flour found their way to waiting customers at Bluff, Mexican Hat, Goulding's Trading Post, Oljeto, Kayenta, Inscription House, Navajo Mountain, Shiprock, Gallup, and many other places.

How well I remember one of those trips. Three days before Christmas I started out with a load of flour for Dennehotso. It had been storming, but by driving all night I reached the village, unloaded the flour, and started right back home. It was pure mud for several miles near Oljeto. The rear axle broke just as it was getting dark. All I could do was stay in the cab all night, while it rained. In the morning I hiked to Goulding's Trading Post in Monument Valley. There was Harry Goulding, starting the motor in his pickup for a trip to Arizona.

"Come along," he said, and gave me a lift to Kayenta. After a short wait at the trading post there, a young couple headed for Monticello gave me a lift in the afternoon. The roads were so muddy and slick by then that we barely made it up Comb Wash Hill, after passing through Mexican Hat. On through Bluff at midnight, we were halfway to Blanding (with the biggest part of the trip behind us) when their car ruptured its oil pan on a sharp rock.

"I'll hike back to Bluff," I said to them with false cheerfulness. It was full morning when I arrived and found Dick Nielson who came out with his truck. With great difficulty, he pulled the car up White Mesa Hill and on to Blanding, where it was repaired. They brought me into Monticello on Christmas afternoon, the fourth day that I had been out with very little sleep. No, I didn't lie down and nap. I got a new axle, rode back with this same couple to the reservation where my truck was stalled, put in the new axle, and drove home once more, 685 miles and almost five days of non-stop activity driving ten to twenty miles an hour.

Thirty years later I used that on-the-spot axle-repairing experience for a guided Jeep tour into Standing Rocks. An axle broke. Luckily, after eight hours, one lonely Jeepster passed on his way out. He took out a message for me. Two days later, pilot Dick Smith flew over from Monticello and dropped a new axle. The Jeep was ready and waiting for it; the broken parts had been removed. The Jeep had its new axle in and was on its way in half an hour ... a major repair job, accomplished in the wilderness with pliers and a wrench.

The high praise of my passenger on that recent trip sounded strange in my ears, since there had never been any expressed admiration for such exploits in the earlier era—thirty years before. What was in a day's work in my youth was accepted without comment by family and community.

In a big storm on another early reservation trip, the truck slid off the road into a drain ditch. I knew it was impossible to get it back on the road while it was loaded. As always in such crises, it was just getting dark. I laid the tailgate on the ground and unloaded my five tons of flour on it. By then the ground had frozen solid. It was possible to get the truck on the road grade and backed up to the flour. All that remained was to reload. The sun was just coming over the hills as I lifted the last sack of flour. I had been at it from sundown to sunup. The flour was delivered by noon, and I drove back immediately to Monticello, arriving home at midnight.

We put over 100,000 miles on that good truck, mostly with me driving, and I enjoyed it. I liked going places and seeing different things. What I couldn't have known at the time was that it was the best possible preparation for my later trail-launching Jeep trips in the canyons. I was learning to get around the country in all kinds of weather conditions on dirt roads, with instant repair and every challenge in vehicle maintenance.

My folks had moved into town permanently. Grandfather Frost stayed at Dodge with me one season. Dad asked us to herd a flock of turkeys. "Herd" is the appropriate word. We actually drove them around the range while they picked up wheat, grasshoppers, and other insects. Grandfather Frost was a good carpenter. He was a better carpenter than a turkey-herder. As we made our rounds he taught me how to whittle whistles from tree saplings and started me carving such things as knife handles, an art I'm happy practicing every winter. He made me a deerskin slingshot and taught me how to use it. He was pleasant, not always lecturing me like my other grandparents.

Trapping was profitable. I spent part of my time riding a black horse to my trap lines all over the mesa and nearby canyons, with coyotes bringing $20, bobcats $10, and foxes $5. On the trail the black horse had a habit of edging far out on the sheer canyon side. I was afraid to kick him too hard, for fear he might jump over. To take my mind off what he was doing, I watched more sharply for prehistoric Indian camps and trails until I could spot them easily. It became more and more interesting to me to come along in the twentieth century and read the signs of those who had been there a thousand years before.

The urge to find my way through unmapped country by following the trails of the ancients and the early cowboys grew.

In March I closed my front door, put on my pack, and hitched to Blanding. I stayed overnight with our family dentist, Dr. Cohen, and rode out the next morning with some miners on their way to the Cottonwood mines. Striking westward on my own, I found my first old horse trail, going down into Comb Wash, and I was in unmapped land.

I felt so lucky that when I came to a bobcat caught in a steel trap I freed him by shooting off the two toes that held him. As he ran out into the sagebrush he looked lucky, too. The trail into Comb Wash was probably the same trail old Posey used when, wounded, he staged his last battle there. I was searching for a horse trail I had heard led over Cedar Mesa. I missed it and ended up on a ridge east of Arch Canyon, beside a beautiful, deep cave, just tall enough for standing. Gathering plenty of wood, I made an excellent camp. It snowed during the night. Next morning I tried to hike from there up Elk Mountain, but the snow grew deeper and deeper. It reached my knees. I was exhausted and discouraged. But as soon as I built a fire under a large ponderosa pine, I slept well. The next day's snow forced me back down into Comb Wash, which I followed to the San Juan River. Hiking through Butler Wash to the old Mormon Trail brought me back to familiar Bluff.

This first venture on my own into a little-known area gave me confidence. I began to hit the trail at every opportunity, taking my gun and slim provisions, and seeking a new canyon each time. I might often be without water or food for a stretch of time. It is a very unusual feeling to lack one of the common commodities of life. Suddenly, when it is found, a man feels very rich and comfortable.

Directions from cowboys led me to unusual places. I found natural arches, Indian paintings, and petroglyphs. There's no end to what is interesting . . . for instance, the wild cows. They have to sop up water from the wet slickrocks when it rains, or lick a thin layer of snow for a drink. They sometimes go five days between drinks. When they reach one, they drink so much that their sides puff out to twice the normal size. They'll trail five miles for food and five miles back for water.

Remote, Mexican Hat, anchored by its great rock sombrero on the banks of the wild San Juan River.

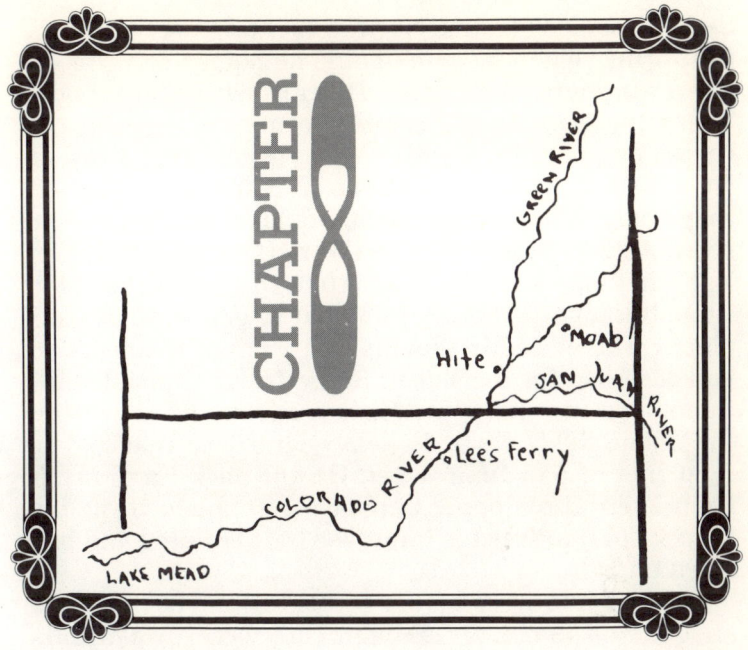

It was my good fortune to meet Norman Nevills at his home in 1935. He was about 31 at the time. After Major Powell's great exploits—descending and exploring the Colorado River in 1869 and 1871—only a sprinkling of river runners had attempted the trip. Norm pioneered in making the adventurous rides safe and popular for ordinary people. He perfected the boats and the system for running the forbidding rapids. He was a topnotch boatman.

When I met Norm the Nevills family comprised almost the total population of Mexican Hat—anchored by its great rock sombrero on the banks of the wild San Juan River, a hot spot in terms of color and temperature.

Norm's father had arrived here in the '20's at the tail end of the oil exploration. The Hat, originally called Goodrich, had been a boom oil town. When the boom ended, the population dropped from several hundred to two, the senior Nevills. Norm was attending college in California. When he came home he helped drill for oil a few summers, then married the girl whose father published the *San Juan Record.* Norm was a geological survey engineer for a while. When he and Jack Frost of New Mexico were government oil inspectors together, they got to wondering what it would be like to run the river. As they studied the shallow riffles near Mexican Hat, they speculated on whether they could develop enough maneuverability in a boat to get through such places. The elder Mr. Nevills told them of the boats he had designed for the Yukon River. Norm copied his father's idea in rough pine gathered from old shacks on the Hat oil fields. He had a heavy, large boat that soaked up plenty of San Juan water. He and Jack Frost ran it from The Hat to Copper Canyon . . . a maiden voyage so successful that it led to improved boat building and polished trips.

Local people were afraid of the river. They thought anyone was foolish to ride on it. They were always making comments about Norm's being crazy, saying that he would be killed and kill other people on the river. Right from the start of my association with him, I, too, was classed as being crazy. That was just the challenge Norm liked.

He was 5'6" and used to say, "Trouble with those big guys is they depend on their brawn, instead of their brain, and they're always in trouble." After experimenting on the San Juan River, he went up to Green River, Wyoming, put in his boats, and went all the way down the Colorado. In spite of the troubles that beset such an adventure, he came through Cataract Canyon and Grand Canyon in good shape, accompanied by a full load of passengers. One distinguished herself by being the first woman ever to make this trip. Named Dr. Clover, she was a botany teacher who took specimens all the way.

"By hell, that's pretty good," was all Norm had to say about his voyage. But the rest of the country was impressed. The national publicity Norm got from that trip made local people revise their opinions. A few even got around to trying a river trip.

When I visited Mexican Hat again, I was delighted to be able to do some carpentry for the man who was gaining fame for his river audacity. I waited for the chance to say, "Mr. Nevills, I'd like to go on one of your river trips."

How pleased I was when he said, "I'll take you, Kent. I think you'd make a good boatman." In 1937 he had a river trip planned on the San Juan. Down I went to Mexican Hat. We worked for about two weeks, constructing a boat with rough, used lumber, scavenged from abandoned Hat oil fields. To my disappointment, the trip did not materialize. His passengers cancelled.

Water is a big attraction for a dry country man. So back I went to Mexican Hat in August of 1938. This time I worked for a week, hauling water from the San Juan River up the hill to pour into a large storage tank at the Mexican Hat Lodge, operated by Nevills' mother. Then we constructed a new boat from Sitka spruce, shipped all the way from Oregon. We also prepared three canvas foldboats 36" x 15' with removable planks that enabled us to collapse and pack the boats compactly for transport. This was the year Norm made his famous long-run trip, and he had just returned. Fresh from his triumphs, he told me so many interesting stories about the big trip as we worked on the boat that I could hardly wait for it to be finished and for us to be on our way.

"I'm the first one," he said, "to take women and children on long river trips."

As the passengers started arriving from all over the country, I felt my responsibility more and more.

"Wonder what they'd think," I said to Norm, "if they knew this was my first experience in handling a boat in swift water."

"Don't worry. You'll do well," he assured me, as he made a last check of his provisions for the five days and reviewed what he had already told me many times.

"Seven dozen eggs ... there won't be as many eddies as in the Grand because of low water, so it's a good place to begin ... 30 loaves of bread ... remember, I'll brief you on each rapids ... we always examine them before running them ... 15 pounds of bacon ... learn how to read the river to avoid submerged boulders ... if thrown out, keep your feet forward by floating on your back, if possible, to prevent crashing head-on into boulders ... five heads of lettuce ... our system is good, with boatmen rowing upstream yet going down river, facing the approaching rapids ... you're in a position to see what's coming ... ten bags of marshmallows ... they're dangerous rivers ... you have to be careful."

That was how he always concluded—with "dangerous river" and how careful you had to be. He was right to emphasize these points, and he was firm in running the rivers in a safe way. No boats ever spilled on a Nevills trip.

We launched from remote, glamorous little Mexican Hat with high expectations, all realized in a thrilling trip. There were two passengers in my boat. I had no trouble. I soon felt very competent at controlling the boat with a pair of oars, as it floated down the racing San Juan current, a glorious adventure for boatmen and passengers.

In those days the muddy San Juan was often a faster river than the Colorado—sometimes as fast as nine miles per hour. The brilliant colors and wild scenery blended with the river's action. The high, vertical walls of the Great Goosenecks snaked us around bend after bend. Rapids like Government, Paiute, and Thirteen-Foot were fearful-looking pieces of water, as they tossed and spit our boats through their boulders. The San Juan River was unique because it had chiselled its way down through a thousand feet of hard limestone formation and cut through at least three huge anticlines.

The low river gave us a tough task many times, when we had to unload the passengers and push the boats over sandbars. Each day there were clouds in the sky, but if it rained anywhere, the water never reached the San

Juan. The river did not rise. The explanation came when we reached its juncture with the Colorado River. That stream was red with floodwater and carried a tremendous amount of debris and driftwood. That's where the run-off was going.

There I was—on the Colorado River in Glen Canyon—a place of wonder and glory.

Our main stop was Forbidden Canyon, with its six-mile hike up to Rainbow Bridge. Nevills called it Forbidden Canyon, referring to certain Indian legends about the place. Later on people who did not understand the legends called it Aztec Canyon because of the small ruins in the entrance. The Bridge was tremendous. I had my first thrilling view of it. Its beautiful arch was like a ribbon of stone across the sky.

It rained all the next day. We had a bunch of cold, wet people when we pulled into camp that night. It was my job to take care of the camp chores, although the two other boatmen, Jack Frost (no relation) and Loren Bell, were kind in helping me. Norm was pleased when I got a roaring fire going quickly.

"How'd you do it with that wet wood?" he asked. I showed him my hatchet.

"I split open enough large willows to get dry kindling." He used to joke about my hatchet. There were so many handy jobs I could do with it. It was the right tool for repairing the Sitka spruce boat, when he split one of the planks on a rock. I used the hatchet to drive caulking into the crack. That handy hatchet also opened cans, carved Moqui steps in the rock (to escape when a few of us were caught high on some slickrock), chopped boughs to make a bed, and—when decently wiped off—served as a meat cleaver.

Because of the low-water stage in the San Juan, we were two days late arriving at Lee's Ferry. For me, the trip wasn't over yet. There was another treat in store. After loading the boats on a trailer, we drove to the south rim for my first view of the Grand Canyon. Locked at the bottom—a mile down—was a tiny thread of river. Hard to believe it was the Colorado I had just traveled so familiarly. I yearned to be back on it. Norm had just run this stretch—and the rest of the river—through Grand Canyon a couple of months before. Gazing at it from the rim, we talked and talked about the river.

"Some day," I was thinking, "I'll be running a boat through there." The vastness and big silence brought back an earlier scene, when I had the same ambitions as a small boy on top of Mt. Peale. Then I had shared the moment with Alfred and Melvin. They were too busy now for adventuring. Alf was committed to farming 300 acres that summer. Mel was attending summer school.

That first San Juan River trip made me a permanent river man. My fondness for rivers and boats has stayed with me ever since, as well as my respect for Norm Nevills. He opened up a new era and world of experience for me. Throughout the following years, I was boatman for his trips down the San Juan, the Snake, and the Salmon, and finally realized my ambition of running Grand Canyon.

If we had energetic photographers aboard for the San Juan run, Norm would send them ahead in my boat to the juncture of the San Juan with the Colorado. We would climb a great wall and walk up a long slope of slickrock, until we were several hundred feet above the river and directly opposite the San Juan's mouth. As the rest of the party came floating into view between those mighty walls, we had a spectacular picture, with the tiny boats approaching the confluence below. Then we would descend and catch up with the group at Hidden Passage Bar for the night's camp.

We customarily hiked up Hidden Passage for a mile to a falls we could climb. In the bend of the falls was an immense, overhanging rock. Halfway up it, a narrow shelf ran around the inside of the overhang. By lying on our stomachs, we could crawl along the shelf, looking down several hundred feet to the sand below. It was a tradition followed on every trip until a tall, slim doctor from Salt Lake found he didn't have enough muscle to work his way around the narrowest part, about thirteen inches wide. He gave out completely and could not move either way until he had rested for a long time. Everyone had worried so much for fear he might slide over the edge of this drop that we abandoned this exercise.

Norm was a daring man, a good climber, and a fine athlete. He started taking passengers up to the top of Rainbow Bridge, even camped up there one night with two others. It was breezy and cold, they said. Once he walked 300 feet on a two-inch cable over the San Juan River. He would pretend to be falling, then catch the cable with his hands and pull himself up. Falling into high water there could have drowned a man. A local drunk tried, at a later date, to copy Norm, fortunately when the water was low. Twenty feet out he fell, so we pulled him out. I was tempted to try it, too. I climbed to the cable car in full moonlight, but made the mistake of watching those big sand waves flooding down the river channel under me. They make a person dizzy. Halfway out I turned back.

I would go down to Mexican Hat during the winter months and help Norm for a week at a time. One year we were drilling a water well for the Lodge. All went smoothly until we got down near the water strata.

"Should be coming up soon," Norm said.

"Here it is," I called, hearing a faint hiss and rumble. Then, "It's oil!"

"Damn!" he said. He was madder 'n hell.

"We'll have to let this one go and get our water some place else." It wasn't a successful well, as far as he was concerned. He said he was through prospecting for oil, and he meant it.

I remember Doris Nevills, Norm's wife, with great admiration. She encouraged me to learn and study at just the time I needed such encouragement. I didn't know much besides dry farming, and she helped me get an education. Since then, each person I've been with for any length of time has been an education in himself. It takes some listening and paying attention.

Summer trips make good winter dreams. On a cold night, the winter after my first San Juan trip, I was carving a new gun handle before the fire, and it began to seem like an oar whose blade needed smoothing to cut the water better. The roar of the fire turned into the roar of a big river's rapids.

"A river trip of my own . . . ," I told myself. Just then my cousin, Ruell Randall, arrived. He was my age and we frequently worked together when he came up from his home in Arizona.

I was living alone at Dodge. My parents had moved into town permanently. The solitary life appealed to me, so I farmed for them. Ruell was a welcome visitor. We sat for a long time before the fire while I described my San Juan boat journey. I don't remember anyone at home being curious about the trip, so, evidently, when I had a captive audience, I exploited it.

"Sounds like something I'd enjoy," said Ruell, hours later. Then he told me about a hike he'd had with Melvin. "Mel took the heels off his shoes to be like the Indians," he said. "When his feet got sore, he had to wrap cowhide around the shoes to build them up again. Walking behind him, I could sure smell those shoes."

I was thinking, "Ruell and I both like to hike. He's interested in the river trips and has met Nevills. He was good company on a couple of reservation flour trips with me." So when August came I took Ruell by surprise.

He was back again at Monticello from Arizona for the summer. We were attending a fathers-and-sons picnic on Blue Mountain.

"Would you like to go on a little hike with me, Ruell?" I asked. He was willing. I had planned for this particular departure, but he hadn't. Earlier that day I had climbed to the nearest peak and figured out the way from Blue Mountain towards the Henrys. How many times before had I climbed a Blue Mountain peak to brood over those distant Henry Mountains? Now I was going to head for them, with a companion.

We simply walked away from the picnic without saying good-bye to anyone in our families. I set our course down from Blue Mountain into Indian Creek. I had the only pack. In it I had stored candy, dried fruit, cornmeal, raisins, matches, and a hatchet. We took turns carrying it. I had 100 bullets with me for my .38 special pistol.

Crossing over West Mountain, we camped the first night at Mormon Pasture Canyon. Next night, we bedded down late on Elk Mountain. Natural Bridges, 75 miles from home, was as far as we could get the third night. The site is extraordinary for having three great natural bridges together. Two of them are so large that each spans the main canyon. They were all formed from the same Cedar Mesa sandstone that covers so much of this country and from which so many wonders have been carved. Arches, Indian caves, hundred of canyons —White Canyon, Fish Creek, Dark Canyon, Grand Gulch, Fable Valley, the Needles, Salt Creek, Horse Canyon, Beef Basin—all eroded from pink and white solidified sand dunes, alternated with bands of red mudstone. The bridges are so white that it's hard to believe they are in the same formation as the rainbow Needles or Dark Canyon. How the ancient Indians must have loved the bridges—Indian ruins are dense in this area.

From the custodian of the bridges, Zeke Johnson, we got a package of rice and a little sugar. The rice went well with stewed rabbit. As we hiked around to examine the bridges, night came, so we camped under Kachina Bridge. The bridges are in White Canyon, and it seemed like a good idea to continue following the canyon the next day. There had been a flood in it a few days before, so there were plenty of potholes of fresh water. But the bottom got too rough. Ruell developed a bad blister on his foot. I cauterized it with hot water.

It seemed best to climb out at Duckett, where following an old horse trail would make easier going. The trouble with that turned out to be that there was no water up there. It was hot and dry. Towards 8 P.M., we stopped to rest and eat a bite. I said, "Let's hike tonight when it's cool." The air was so refreshing at 2 A.M. that it wasn't hard to get up and start out again. We got along fine until midday. Then, hot and thirsty, we napped under a juniper tree. At that point it was possible to re-enter White Canyon and again use the bottom. Seven miles later, the same day, in the midst of plunging landscapes and rising cliffs, backed by towering mountains, we reached the Colorado shores.

It was beautiful. Three canyons met at Hite: Farley and White almost came together where we stood; Trachyte was on the other side. Beaches touched the cliffs on our side, farm bottoms on the other. Green trimmed the tall, red walls: green willows, grasses, shrubs. A blue heron flew by. Coming to an abandoned prospector's camp, we searched it.

"More supplies," we chortled, holding up a quart bottle full of cracked wheat and a small amount of chocolate in a can.

"This is a good place to build our raft," I suggested. Ruell hadn't known I meant a river trip until we arrived at Hite where Glen Canyon began. I could swim, but he couldn't. I told him it was the quietest part of the river.

It was a gratifying mark of his confidence that he agreed calmly. He must have figured I knew what I was doing. It didn't take long to choose driftwood logs from a big pile and tie them together with pieces of old rusty cable that were lying around the shore.

"Are we done?" Ruell asked. "Is this it?" Maybe it wasn't much, but it looked great to us. We watched a tree branch sail down the center of the river.

"About three miles an hour," Ruell guessed. "That'll be our speed."

"Well?"

"Well?" Then our eyes met.

"All right," I said, "let's shove off. If we don't make it, we'll always think we should have."

The logs held together as we bobbed through the Hite "rapids." We were whooping and hollering with our success. We floated on for a mile, our handmade raft carried along by a two-block-wide river in the wilderness.

"What's that ahead?" asked Ruell.

"A water wheel!" we said together. It was turning in the river current. We pulled ashore to see it. Down came a man, then his wife, and then their two sons.

"Hey," said one, "where you goin' on that thing?"

"Down the river on this *raft*," we said with dignity.

"How far?"

"Lee's Ferry." We noticed the father exchange looks with the mother.

"We're surprised," we added. "We weren't expecting to see a family living down here."

"No more surprised than we are at seeing you. We've been living here about six months, placer mining for gold. We're not the only ones here. Why don't you cross the river and talk with Arthur Chaffin? He has a fine ranch there, and he knows more about Glen Canyon than anybody alive."

Before we could come to a decision of our own about it, we found our little raft beached and one of the Gerhart boys rowing us across in their family boat. Mr. Chaffin was just as surprised to see us as the family on the other shore had been. He was about 45 years old on that first visit in 1940.

"Where did you come from, boys? What are your names? What are your plans?"

We discovered that he knew my father. When he learned that we were planning to float through Glen Canyon on a raft, he was very concerned.

"Now why don't you stay here for a week?" he suggested. "You can work for me, and I'll pay you by building you a small boat which would be much safer. You'll get to Lee's Ferry just as soon, because it's quicker to row a boat than just float on a raft with the current."

We were reluctant. We wanted to be on our way. Many years later I learned that the Gerhart family's son had been sent to tell him our raft was very unstable and dangerous. I'm willing to admit now that it probably was. Mr. Chaffin finally convinced us, so we put our pitifully tiny pack of supplies on a corner of his porch and went in to meet his wife. She seemed surprised to see us, too, but gave us a friendly welcome and sent us to wash for the meal she was ready to put on the table. She surely was a good cook, and their ranch was a marvel.

That place called Hite was as far as you could be from civilization . . . on the wild Colorado River, deep down between the highest walls of canyons that had to be followed to their heads, 80 miles east or 50 miles west, to meet any other permanent dweller. Yet they had all kinds of fresh fruits and vegetables, and urged us to feel free to help ourselves. The Chaffins had olive, fig, apricot, and apple trees, grain crops, grapes, horses with excellent stables, pigs in fine pens, and a Ford car.

Everything Mr. Chaffin built was solid and well-designed—his house, his fence, his water system. Carpentry was one of his loves. He had a large building devoted to it. Workbenches lined the long walls. Neatly organized cabinets held every kind of tool, nail, and bolt. He was clever about designing equipment to do a job. He had figured out a saw arrangement of his own. There was a forge in a corner, with a steam engine and boiler to run the power tools.

The more we worked there, the more we liked the ranch and admired the Chaffins. He started us hoeing weeds in the garden. I did not like hoeing weeds very much, but I thought I was doing it with good grace. Years later he told me, "Your cousin was doing fine on that hoeing, but I could see that your heart wasn't in it. You were ready to take off on that raft again. I had to think of something else to keep you there." He asked if we knew anything about mechanical work.

"I've been raised on the homestead. I repair our farm equipment and cars," I said.

"Good," he answered. "I have a 1926 Dodge across the river that we can fetch over, if you'll work on it." He took his two rowboats, with an outboard motor on the back of one, and two 3 X 12 planks across the river. We pumped up the tires on the old Dodge with a hand pump, then pushed the car over the sand to the river's edge. By lining it up with the planks we were able to put it sideways across the boats, then lash it down solidly with ropes. We ferried the car uneventfully across the river. Horses pulled it up the hill into the yard.

River water had corroded the motor. Our seven days of work were almost up by the time we had taken every piece of it apart, cleaned each with steam pressure from a hot steam boiler in the shop, then washed each one with gasoline.

"Let's knock off now," Mr. Chaffin said, "and see if we can get the boat made."

From a pile of rough lumber, he took two 1 X 12 planks; we bent them around some ribs that had been laid together with 2 X 4's. In three hours we had the boat completed. While Mr. Chaffin put on the boards, Ruell and I were stuffing rags in the cracks and pouring tar over them. We loaded the boat on the wagon, hauled it down to the river, and put it in to soak for the night.

Our supplies were still in the corner of the porch where we had put them a week ago. We picked them up in the morning and added to them a gift from the Chaffins—a dozen guinea hen eggs and several large watermelons. As we stepped into the boat, Art Chaffin said to me, "Does your family know where you are?"

"I doubt it very much."

"Then you sit right down here and write them a postcard. I'm going to Hanksville tomorrow and will mail it." I could hardly have known that my family was less worried about me before than after receiving the card. The thought of my boating on the Colorado left them without hope for me.

As the days and weeks piled up after the card came, my younger sister, Pearl, would weep, "I know he's drowned. I just know it," and my mother did not console her convincingly.

The Gerharts also came down to see us off. "Goodbye," they called from one shore, as the Chaffins called from the other.

"Have a good trip."

A pair of oars we had chopped from poles worked well on our small boat. We were on our way to run the length of Glen Canyon. It had taken only two weeks to achieve my objective.

It wasn't long before we discovered that the cracked wheat, found at the prospector's camp, was full of weevils. The can of chocolate was the bitter kind. This meant that once the eggs and watermelon were gone, there wasn't going to be much to eat. On the third day I stood up in the boat.

"There's beaver, Ruell. Our dinner." I missed him by 6 inches. A minute later he surfaced about 75 yards away. I shot again and hit him right in the ear. Beavers swim along with only the ears exposed, so this was a perfect hit. I rowed the boat to the bloody spot in the water where he had sunk and dived overboard. When I could feel him, I clamped the beaver between my feet and brought him up with me.

"Pretty good," Ruell said. "Now we eat." We made camp for the night, boiled beaver slices in a can, and got ready for a big feast. What a disappointment. It tasted so strongly of willows and mud, and was so extremely tough, that we could hardly chew it, much less swallow it. It made Ruell sick.

"Let's try using it for bait," Ruell suggested. We found that catfish liked beaver meat very much. We were pulling a catfish out about every five minutes. As soon as one was caught, we killed it, cleaned it, and laid it on the coals to cook. It must have been hours before we stopped catching, cooking, and eating catfish. With contented sighs we stretched out on Grissman Bar and let sleep overpower us. We kept the rest of the beaver meat and fished successfully from the boat for days after that.

"What's that?" Ruell asked, pointing to what looked like a large canyon on the left. I could hardly recognize it as the San Juan River. It was completely dry. We hiked up it a short distance, then returned and camped across from its mouth that night. Thirty years later I was able to show my companions on a different raft trip the initials I carved high in the wall there on the first journey.

We were sightseers at Music Temple six miles later, and then reached the mouth of the Escalante River where I carved initials in stone for the second and last time anywhere in the wilderness. I admit it was a thrill to find them again 31 years later.

"How do you like it, Ruell?" I asked, when we halted at Hole-in-the-Rock. He hadn't said much, and I was beginning to wonder.

"It surely is a pretty place. I like the sand beaches. To a dry-land boy from Arizona, the river looks mighty big to me."

"It looks big to people from water spots, too," I told him. We both thought Glen Canyon was beautiful and rejoiced that we were there. We both hushed and stopped rowing. We both saw them at the same time ... a doe and two fawns at the river's edge. The current was carrying us so silently they did not see us until we were exactly opposite them. I still recall their surprised expression.

When we saw a man standing on shore the first day,

we pulled in to talk to him. He was hiking up to see the Chaffins, planning to return by boat. Everyone hiked upstream, floated down; no one could fight the Colorado's current. He looked so hot and tired that we gave him some watermelon slices. His name was Bud Vinger. Our favor was returned by three miners at Hansen Creek, farther on, who invited us to join them in a dinner of beef and venison. The miners had wondered how reliable our little boat was. We wished they could have seen it the next day. We bounced over sand waves caused by a flood that carried huge amounts of silt and came out of Bullfrog Canyon. Art Chaffin had built us a worthy craft.

We floated up to the mouth of Forbidden Canyon—my second visit, Ruell's first. We hiked in. I kept the big sight a surprise. Ruell thought Rainbow Bridge was a marvel and enjoyed it as thoroughly as I enjoyed introducing him to it.

"It's the world's largest natural stone bridge," I told him. "309 feet high inside this arch."

"It must be the least known, too," he replied, tallying the names on the register to which we had just added ours. Less than a thousand visitors had traveled to see Rainbow Bridge from the time of its discovery in 1909 to that day in July, 1939 . . . an average of 32 people a year.

"I can see why it's sacred to the Navajo Indians," I said with my head tipped back 45 degrees to admire the tapering top. "They never walk through it, you know, always around it."

We had not explored many side canyons on that trip. Side canyons used to be one of the glories of Glen Canyon. Like most boys, we were concentrating on the mechanics and motion of the journey. All those miles from Hite to Lee's Ferry took us seven days. At noon we pulled our boat far up on the bank at Lee's Ferry. Our enormous river adventure was ended. We had no further use for the boat, but had grown so fond of it that we could not bear to leave it without beaching it properly.

We still had the problem of returning home. A four-mile hike on a very hot afternoon brought us to Marble

Canyon Lodge. We bought a loaf of bread, a jar of jam, and a bottle of pop. From then on we had 500 miles to hitchhike. The hitching was undependable. The hiking must have totaled at least a hundred of those miles. We worked at it for five days. Ruell had hated to leave the boat, and with good reason.

At Kanab I led us up to the door of Aunt Annie Frost's home. I had not seen her since the days of the '27 trip in our Dodge touring car. When I asked her if we could stay overnight, Aunt Annie looked us over. Our clothes showed that we had been sleeping by the fire in them for three weeks.

"All right, boys," she said, steering us towards the bathroom. "March right in there and scour yourselves. Dinner will be ready pretty soon." It was a fine dinner, and we slept in a bed that night. Good Aunt Annie.

At Richfield we asked the sheriff to let us sleep in the jail because it was cold and rainy.

"How old is this boy?" he demanded, pointing his finger at my cousin. Ruell was 17. (I must have looked aged.)

"I cannot let anyone under 18 sleep in the jail. Sorry, boys, it will be impossible to let you in tonight." At the edge of town we burrowed into a fresh haystack for the night.

A few open-air, wet truck rides brought us into Price the next day, where we searched the south side of town looking for the hobo jungle or a place to get in out of the rain. There was no hobo hangout. Between us we dug 45 cents out of our pockets and persuaded a lady motel operator to let us sleep in a slightly used cabin she had not yet made up.

Just recently Ruell told me, "When we split up at Price the next morning—that's when I was the most scared of the whole trip." Splitting up was my suggestion, because I thought it would be easier to get rides separately. A preacher from New Mexico picked me up. Soon we caught up with Ruell who had gone ahead.

"That's my cousin, there, and he is a fine fellow, too," I said. "Would you like to take him?" He did, and the three of us rode into Monticello. Ruell and I arrived a little over one month from the day we walked away from the Blue Mountain picnic. Our families seemed glad to see us, but I have never been able to recall anyone's asking for details of that wonderful journey.

CHAPTER 10

After that I made at least one trip to Hite every year. I was devoted to Mr. Chaffin and liked to be with him at every opportunity. He called me son. One year, when I yearned to return to Hite as early as possible, mine was the first auto over Elk Mountain as the snows thawed. Arriving at the river, I found the ferry had been swept away by the high spring floods. All that remained was a cable stretching an eighth of a mile from shore to shore, with two large pulleys, their broken wires streaming from them at the cable's center. There was no boat on the other side. Impatiently, I embarked on my toughest crossing of that rowdy river.

Hooking my tow-chain over the cable, I secured a two-foot board in it for a seat and started to slide the hook along the cable. It was easy going towards the center because of the steep incline. But when I reached the middle, my feet dragged in the ice-cold water. I had arrived at the pulleys and their streaming wires. To transfer from one side of them to the other, I had to lock an arm over the main cable and lift the hook and chain which weighed about fifteen pounds. Working along the upgrade for the second half became more and more difficult as I approached the anchorage. But two hours' effort brought me to the opposite shore, 700 feet from my start.

Mr. and Mrs. Chaffin and another couple arrived in time to be spectators.

"Kent," they said, "we thought it was impossible." But I thought that Hite was worth that much effort. How I loved Hite, with its verdant green ranch at the bottom of a redrock bowl. I loved the beautiful cliffs rising on every side, and the muddy river, doggedly streaming by, dragging everything believable and unbelievable in its torrent and grinding it up. I thought of Hite as a second home. When I left at the end of the week, Mr. Chaffin asked me to come back to help him build a new ferry.

Two weeks later, when I returned, I took an easier crossing. A boat came for me. With two other men we constructed the second Hite ferry, a large barge made of 2 X 8 planks. Out close to the edge of the barge, in the river with Chaffin, I spread out my tools to prepare for some hammering and sawing. "Better tie those tools to you or the boat, son." he said. "This old river will take everything from you it can get." Oh, that water was swift.

The Hite ferry, Mr. Chaffin's original idea, was the only link that connected one half of southern Utah with the other half, split as they were by the Colorado River. The state had finally acceded to Chaffin's plea—for a ferry with roads leading to it from Hanksville and Blanding—on the condition that he build and maintain the ferry. He kept his word under the most trying conditions. On this occasion, when the barge was finished and on her maiden voyage, the outboard motor that was pushing her died in midstream. Chaffin struggled out there for two hours to put it back in action. We returned to the same shore, and he had another week's work setting up a power winch for crossing. Several years later a new flood tore this one loose, and it also was lost down the river. The state helped construct the third one from war surplus bridge pontoons, a serviceable ferry that lasted until Lake Powell partially filled up.

Another year my dog, Skippy, came along to Hite. He was a big, ill-tempered creature who was as willing to bite a person as leave him alone. Skippy was a gift from Norm. Skippy was at his best on the coupe's back shelf with his chin resting on my shoulder as I drove. A family with a beautiful daughter had moved to Hite. I admired her very much. Her Mexican boy friend resented me. One evening as I was returning to my camp near the Cass Hite inscription, he appeared from behind a boulder with a friend. I knew their intention was to beat me up. But Skippy beside me growled like a mad dog; his hair stood on end. He sounded as though he were ready to eat them. Indeed, if I had not held on to his collar, he might have. They changed their minds, left instantly, and later decided to become friends. Our rivalry was wasted. The beautiful daughter married a third man.

"I'd like to see this Hite you're always talking about," said Alf.

"Come along," I urged. I would be proud to introduce each to the other.

Alf went to Hite with me in March. We hiked westward from Blanding, approximately along the route that is now Highway 95, and reached Hite in three days. . . 80 miles. The Gerharts were still there and happy to row us across. Up to Chaffin's ranch we went and stayed overnight. This time Chaffin had a large powerboat with a Model A Ford car sitting in the middle of it for power and a paddle wheel attached to each side. His only difficulty was that this boat was down at Red Canyon with a broken drive shaft. He wondered if we would like to go down with him to repair the boat, then journey on to Grissman Bar and help with some assessment work on mining claims.

We floated downriver in a rowboat with the spare parts; soon we reached the paddle wheel job, repaired it, and chugged on luxuriously to Grissman Bar. After several days' work on the mining claims we were camped at Red Canyon on the way back, when Mr. Chaffin asked if we had ever climbed to the top of Mount Ellsworth. That sounded like a good adventure, so Alf and I left him to hike up Tickaboo Canyon and right on up to the top of the southernmost Henry Mountain.

The wind was blowing so hard up there we had to crouch down among the boulders as we moved along the crest towards Four-Mile Canyon. The cold wind changed our minds about camping out on the peak. We kept on hiking. Just as it was getting dark we reached the canyon. We were lucky to find a slope we could negotiate over those sheer Wingate ledges. Once we got to the river it seemed silly to stop, so we continued hiking the remaining four miles to Hite, arriving back at the ranch at 9:30 P.M. The Chaffins were astonished to see us. They thought it out of the question to hike that far in one day. So did we, especially since Mt. Ellsworth, one of the Henry Mountains discovered by Major Powell, is over 8200 feet high.

Alf found he also liked Hite and the Chaffins, so we lingered for several days, puttering with some of the ranch's mechanical work. When Mr. Chaffin told us he was driving out to Hanksville, Alf decided to take advantage of the ride. But memories of my earlier 500-mile hitchhike made me say, "If you'll just put me across the river, I'll walk home." They did, and I hiked to Blanding in two and a half days, caught a ride from Blanding to Monticello, and arrived ten minutes before my brother did.

Over the next few years I divided my time between dry farming at Dodge, running boats for Nevills, visiting the Chaffins at Hite, and always hiking, exploring farther and farther into the absolute wilderness.

I was now a regular boatman for Norm and went with him on many trips down the San Juan River. The big trips of one year were running the Snake and Salmon Rivers. It seemed as though the whole town of Salmon City, Idaho, turned out to see us shove off, with a few doubters cheering us on.

"I'll bet a dollar you don't make it."

We used three of the closed cataract-type boats and one open San Juan boat, all controlled by the boatman's use of heavy oars. The San Juan was an open boat made of heavy plywood. The cataract boats were enclosed, with 7 airtight compartments and hatch covers. The second afternoon, I was in camp with one other boatman and a lady passenger when an old character strolled into camp wearing a large hat and long, swirling mustaches. At the sight of him, the lady said, "Oh, I'll bet you're the sheriff."

"No, lady," answered the character in a gruff voice, "I'm the bootlegger."

The other boatman, hearing him, announced, "I'm a bootlegger, too."

Evidently there was an exchange of merchandise, as our boatman got drunk that night, to say nothing of the next day. He let his boat drift off course and over some rocks. One of his passengers fell out.

Norm was extremely upset. He went through the boatman's boat, searching for the liquor. He couldn't find it, so he searched the other boats. No liquor. Finally he searched his own and found, cannily hidden in his own storage bin, three bottles which immediately flew into the river and crashed against the boulders. The drunken boatman wailed that he couldn't get along without his nourishment. Norm reprimanded him publicly and severely, and everything was fine from then on down the rest of the river.

It always seemed that local sheriffs and peace officers were playing a good game with the bootleggers during the days of Prohibition. There seemed to be a general knowledge of the people who were making whiskey and selling it. Once in a while the sheriff would arrest a man for selling whiskey, but he was never able to find the whiskey-making equipment. A long-retired bootlegger recently illuminated this puzzle. He told me that the sheriffs would make a point of warning that a raid was planned by saying, "Well, I have to go over there hunting horses in a few days. Have to check up on stolen horses." That gave the bootlegger time to pack up his manufacturing equipment and move it to a new spot. No one really wanted to run him out of business, but just to fine him a bit. Bootleggers' fines were a good source of revenue for counties with lean budgets where there was very little taxable property, most of it being owned by the Federal Government. So it was a general practice to catch the same men over and over.

Prohibition days also brought some wild dances to the little ranching areas. The sports would ride their horses or drive a team ten miles to a dance. They cached their favorite bottles out in back, to spare the sheriff the trouble of arresting them. Everybody knew the favorite bootlegger, whose most popular item was a really good home-brewed beer. Sometimes we boys would hear about a dance, go up there and steal a bottle or two from the cowboys' cache, then try it out.

I refuse to say which uncle left the ranch with me and my brother at 4 A.M. one morning to go deer hunting. I didn't understand the reason for leaving so early, but we had an automobile then and stopped to pick up another man at his ranch. This man spent some time tearing around in the oak brush leaves behind his house, then finally left with us. Before we reached our hunting grounds my uncle and his companion were both drunk. Later my brother and I figured out that we had stopped to visit (and pick up) my uncle's favorite bootlegger. The men didn't get any deer that day.

Once the liquor was eliminated from the Salmon run, we finished without difficulty. The Snake River was much larger. Our only problem was that the open San Juan boats kept filling with water, and we had to keep bailing.

Coming from some wild and untouched rivers, we were mildly surprised at the publicity the Salmon and Snake had received. The Salmon had a big sign on shore saying, "You are now entering the Salmon River primitive area." An auto road ran alongside our route all the way; there were horse trails on both sides; one horse bridge crossed the river and cabins appeared every mile.

Local people claimed Hell's Canyon on the Snake was deeper than Grand Canyon. After checking a map, we guessed they must have gone back several miles to the top of a mountain to start measuring elevation.

As his business increased, Norm decided to prepare camps ahead of time for the river season. We spent three early spring weeks the following year working our way down the San Juan and Colorado to establish the camps. At Slickhorn Canyon we built a trail from the boat landing to some overhanging ledges just above several beautiful pools. We carried a large supply of wood up from the river. It was such a fine spot that others had chosen it long ago; there were names of early expeditions carved into the ledgerock.

The river was at low-level stage. It was strenuous, maneuvering through the many sandbars in icy water. Paiute Farms, a wide, shallow stretch half a mile below Grand Gulch, was where the boat stuck once too often. Paiute Farms was always a big river problem because the river spread out wide there after emerging from narrow canyons, so that the water was too shallow for the boats to float. They invariably got stuck in the sand. We were too tired this time to push our craft off the sandbar it chose to perch on. So we sat for several hours on dry land right there in the middle of a river half a mile wide. We consoled ourselves by eating our lunch. A change in wind, rain, and water level finally helped us off.

Our next construction job was planned for Hidden Passage Bar in Glen Canyon. Arriving there, we made an elaborate storage bin by digging a deep pit in the ground and lining it with lumber salvaged from piles of driftwood. Norm's plan was to cache food there that was taken from the boats while the water was high and running the river was easy. Then the boats on the shallow runs would not have to be so heavily laden. It looked like an ideal square bin, with a door on top, well protected from animals and river floods. What we had failed to protect it from, we learned sadly later, was other river parties who found it and exploited its contents.

One evening we were surprised to hear a motorboat coming up the river. Harry Aleson and Art Green arrived in a tiny aluminum boat. They pulled in beside our boat and camped with us. Apparently this was Art Green's first trip up Glen Canyon.

Camping on beautiful sandbars was always one of the

Shallow Paiute Farms on the San Juan River near Clay Hills Crossing.

specialties of the river trips. But some canyons provided remarkable caves for camping. At Forbidden Canyon we carried boatloads of driftwood into the great cave at the canyon's mouth and built a comfortable camp there. We prepared another food-cache bin. Again at Sentinel Rock we carried wood into Outlaw Cave. While there we were again surprised by a motorboat coming up river. This time it was a young fellow with a large dog, on his way to do some placer mining claim assessments. Traffic was increasing. We wondered if the river was getting too crowded.

In spite of freeloaders, Norm's plan proved to be a good one and helped the season's trips run smoothly.

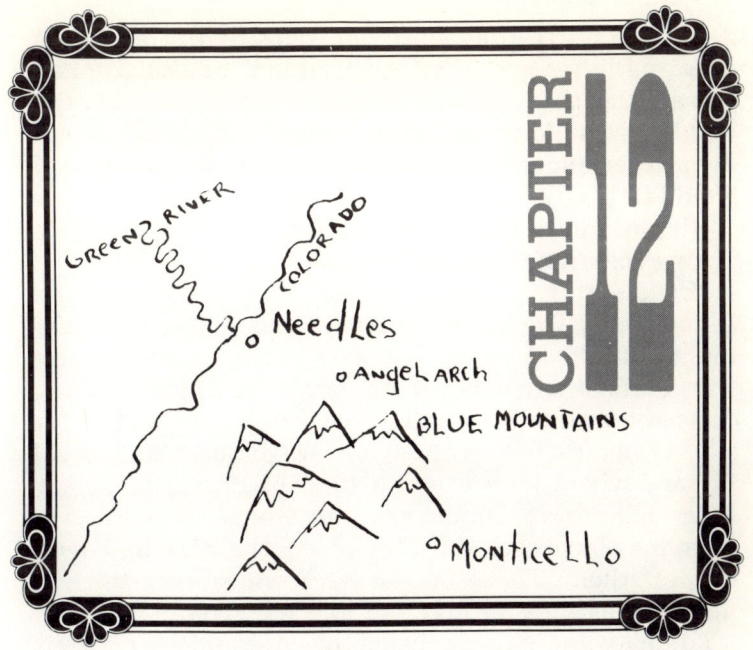

CHAPTER 12

For a long time the Needles had been calling me. But it wasn't until the spring of 1940 that I made up my mind to get in there and investigate what the cowboys had been telling me all my life.

Knowing they made trips from Dugout Ranch, 35 miles from Monticello, I caught a ride to Dugout with one of them, A. Helquist. He was not as surprised that I was going in to see the Needles as he was that I would do it with a simple backpack. Who traveled the Needles without a good horse and full saddlebags?

Dugout was the cowboys' headquarters in Indian Creek, with the only permanent stream in the entire Needles country. I stayed up late, listening to another cowboy, Bill Shupe. He talked to me for hours in the bunkhouse about trails and finding different places in the Needles. It was valuable information, I knew, but it all began to sound the same and was making me bleary.

I wasn't used to following trails then, so it was hard to picture what Bill said. Even in later years, when I had developed my trailing ability, it was still difficult to understand other people's trail terminology. What I had learned by then, however, was to read between the words and build up an image of the trail based on my own experience. Then, with a few simple questions, I would be ready to seek the new trail.

Hiking from Dugout the next day, I reached Cave Spring for my first night's camp.

"Cave Spring." I said it out loud. The cowboys' station for 60 years. The place I had heard them mention over many childhood years. I looked around: wood neatly stacked for their next arrival; precious water dripping down the wall into a small reservoir; large grain box for storing horse's feed, and several wagonloads of hay, all in back where they would always be dry. Several *metates* and *manos,* Indian grinding stones, were lying in what may have been the same places their original owners left them. There on the back walls were the red pictographs the cowboys had told me about.

I didn't want to camp inside the cave and use up their wood. Wouldn't the cowboys be unhappy if they came riding in from a snowstorm and found they had to gather more? Near the cave was an overhang with plenty of fuel. I chose that and slept by my fire.

My direction was right the next morning, when I started out, but I missed the horse trail over Elephant Hill. I was just half remembering what Bill Shupe had told me. I said to myself, as I had to many times then and in the years following, "I'm lost, but I'll go as far as I can this way. If I get stuck, I can always find my way back."

And then those Needles appeared. From a distance they looked like a city skyline. I crossed two deep canyons. As I plodded towards the Needles they began to look like the fingers of hundred of hands. Then I reached the bases of the first ones.

My head tilted back to scan their tops. They were immense stone columns. I was attracted by the crevices at their bases and soon started climbing through them . . . in and out, around, and part way up and part way down. It was fun.

The wonder of the place was growing. These mighty pillars in different sizes and shapes formed solid walls —sculptured spindles, mushroom rocks, thin pillars, fat ones, thousands of them. They were beautiful, in layers of pink, tan, chocolate.

All day I passed them. They enclosed grassy valleys. Later I learned that they had developed from massive uplifts which left cracks, permitting wind and rain to erode them into their present fantastic spires.

In one valley I came upon the horse trail again. I was able to follow it right through to Devil's Lane. What a contrast to the Needles was Devil's Lane—an odd straight corridor. I decided to camp in Devil's Lane that second night.

To clear my campground I had to scrape up a good deal of snow (it was an inch deep in places). Then I melted the snow to use as water for drinking, cooking, and washing. My fire was near some large boulders. During the night, when it began to snow again, the snow that landed on the boulders melted from the fire's heat. To protect my fire I placed cans under the drips. In the morning I found that I had collected a plentiful supply of fresh water, and I had learned a new trick. Ever since then I have caught dripping water from ledges, boulders, crevices . . . whatever is available.

In that land of confusion, the first time I passed through a crevice and moved along the new canyon to which it led me I realized it was nearly impossible to decide *which* crevice had been my route between *which* two spires out of hundreds. I panicked slightly, then discovered that I could use the La Sal Mountains as a guidepost.

It took a few minutes the next morning to locate the La Sals. They looked different. They were snow-covered.

"What have I done?" I thought. "If those are the La Sals, I'm going in the wrong direction."

I scaled a pinnacle that offered easy finger- and toe-holds, to look around. There were two sets of mountains. It was the snowcapped Henrys whose viewing zone I had entered late yesterday. The La Sals remained in their right place, but it was hard to see them because of a cloud cover.

Relaxed now that I was relocated, I began to appreciate the beauty of the Needles. The spires were remarkable with their snowcaps and ribbons. Red and pink sandstone was showing through the glistening white. The piñon and juniper, scattered around their bases and across the bottom of the canyon, showed dark green through the snow mantle. Winter's touch adds to the glamor of the Needles. Few visitors have seen them in their winter beauty.

As I hiked along that day all the ground on the sunny side was bare. There was plenty of snow on the shady side. It started snowing, lightly at first, then heavier. I found a small cave, lit a fire, and sat in my entrance overlook, watching the big flakes simmer down on the spires. As the snow increased it blotted out the opposite wall of the canyon, like a curtain coming down.

The next day I hiked across Beef Basin and over the ridge into Fable Valley, arriving there as it started getting dark. I was lucky to find a large cave—and doubly lucky because in my hand was a rabbit that I had shot with my .38 pistol. I made a trip down to the creek for water and put the rabbit on to boil. Coyotes were howling up and down the canyon. A hoot owl chimed in. Several Indian cliff dwellings could be seen near the creek in the dusk. It was an eerie place. I did not leave my fire all night.

I wanted to get into Dark Canyon, but when I looked into it from the rim the next morning, the snow was a foot and a half deep. That's hard walking. My food supplies were very low. I spotted a large buck. I thought I was close enough to have him in range, and I fired—but I merely wounded him in his hind leg. I started following his trail through the snow but could never get close enough to kill him.

It was again the end of a day, and I was so tired I couldn't walk any farther. I made my camp underneath a large piñon tree. The only shovels I had were my feet. I kicked away about a foot of snow to clear the ground

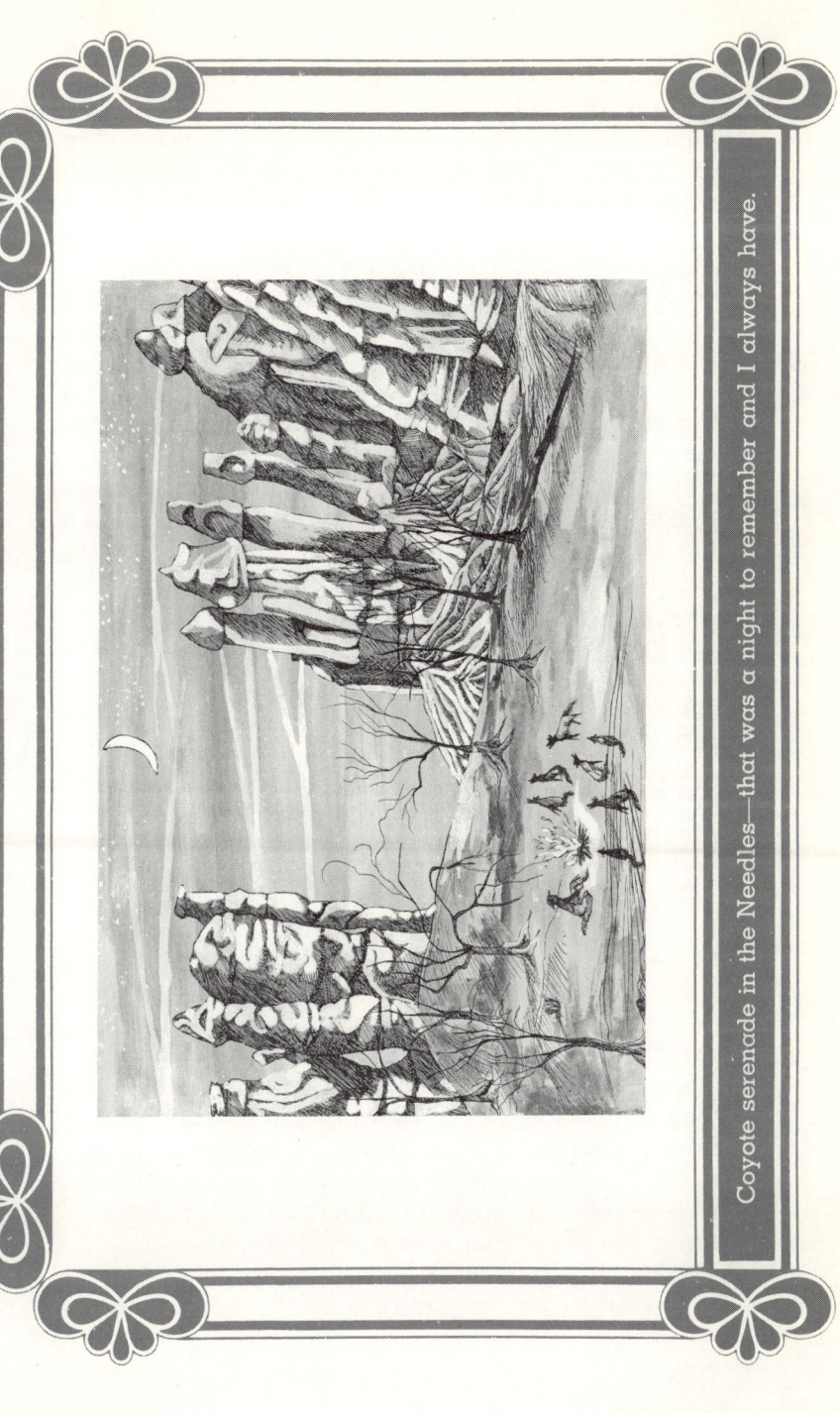

Coyote serenade in the Needles—that was a night to remember and I always have.

for my campfire. It was not more than five miles from my camp of the night before, but it was 1,000 feet higher. Piñon boughs, piled high, made an attractive bed on the frozen ground. I dug out a great pile of wood from the snow and laid it near the fire. Things began to look cozy.

While I was preparing my camp I heard a pack of coyotes chasing the wounded deer. I could tell they had killed him when they quieted down. I cooked my small dinner of cornmeal, raisins, and hot tea, thinking how I would have enjoyed a deer steak for dinner—but I wasn't going down there in the dark to fight with the coyotes about it. My bough bed was calling me. I lay down by the fire and quickly fell sound asleep.

Suddenly, in the middle of the night, it seemed that a coyote was howling right in my ear. I jumped up with my .38 in one hand and my hatchet in the other, thinking the coyotes were going to attack me. I reached over and put more wood on the fire. The coyotes had encircled my camp. They were just barely outside the firelight. I couldn't see them, but, oh! they were close—not more than fifty feet away.

There I was, tired, alone. Although everyone hears tales of wolves attacking, I had always heard that coyotes didn't attack people. But when you're in the position I was that night, you're not certain of anything. I thought I had done them a real good turn by giving them their dinner. But when they came and serenaded me, I was no longer sure. They howled around me for fifteen minutes. Then suddenly all was quiet again. I sat there feeding my fire for a long time. I had to keep assuring myself that it wasn't a nightmare. They had all started up at the same second and quit at the same second. I had to keep reminding myself that my gun had been ready and that I had planned to shoot. It just seemed so unreal, it was hard to believe it was happening. Finally I lay down and fell asleep again—remarkably soundly, considering. But then, that was my fourth night out, and I was getting pretty weary.

I was glad to see the daylight. There was no sign or

sound of the coyotes in the morning. A fresh snowfall had covered their tracks. I wondered how many there had been. Even two or three can sound like a whole pack, but the volume of noise I heard must have come from more. I've often asked myself why I didn't pepper the whole hillside with bullets, but it has always been my policy not to shoot unless I can see what I'm shooting at.

It had been a cold night. My coat felt queer. I took it off to examine it. What a peculiar shape! I had hugged the fire so closely that the black horse-leather had shrunk across the back and shoulders. That was a night to remember, and I always have.

After breakfast I walked the short distance to the rim of Dark Canyon once more and looked in again. It seemed miles deep, with many different ledges covered with snow. I realized it would be impossible to climb down over them and reach the bottom. Discouraged anyway by a hard night, a food shortage, and the deep snow, I turned around to retrace my route home. It took two days to hike back to Elephant Hill.

When I reached the small spring at the foot of the hill I stopped for lunch, which, to no one's surprise, consisted of dry cornmeal and raisins. I drank from the animals' trough to get my water. It was a warm, sunny afternoon. I felt drowsy as I continued down the trail. Almost asleep, I was passing a large juniper tree when suddenly a coyote's howl came from behind it. Jerked awake and a-quiver, I pulled out my pistol and pointed it towards the tree. Then I heard someone snorting, "Ha, ha, ha."

Roy Musselman, the trapper, was standing beside the tree laughing at me. This was the best joke he had had all winter, scaring me half to death. He did not know how close he came to getting shot. After we talked a few minutes he asked, "Hey there, Kent, where are you going to sleep tonight?" I told him I intended to sleep at Cave Spring. Roy suggested that I go to Lost Canyon and dine with him in Lost Cave. His invitation sounded very good to me. He told me to just follow his horse tracks.

They would lead me to Lost Cave. He would be there in a couple of hours.

At Lost Cave I found sourdough biscuits, jam, and coffee waiting for me. This cowboy coffee, I have learned, is quite unusual. The cowboys always use a pot about ten times the size that is necessary; they never dump out the grounds until the pot gets almost full of them. The pot is always sitting in the hot embers ready for pouring.

Soon Roy arrived. He fried up a Dutch oven full of deer meat, and filled another Dutch oven with sourdough biscuits. Washed down with the cowboy coffee, it was one of the most enjoyable meals I have ever eaten. We cleaned up the dishes and sat by the fire for several hours as he told me of the many large wolves, mountain lions, and bears that he had trapped in San Juan County. Roy used to camp at Mormon Pasture in the summertime. He trapped lions and coyotes when he was up in the high mountain range.

"Once," related Roy, "my partner, Jim, came into camp there with a pickup truck. He noted all the tin cans lying out in front and thought he'd do me a favor. So he loaded them in his pickup and hauled them into a wash, where he dumped them. When I come back that night, I says, 'Jim, what the hell did you do with the tin cans?' When Jim tells me he just hauled them to the wash and dumped them, I says, 'Well, we just have to haul ourselves down and find them. I had $1,100 cached in one.'"

So they went down into the wash and, after scrounging through cans for an hour, they found the one with the eleven hundred dollars in it. The story had to be true. More than once, the bank people remarked crustily that he didn't think his little savings were safe with them.

When I told him of my night with the coyotes, he said,

"Oh, that's some of them dang halfbreeds from that female wolf I never could catch." He had a record for catching wolves, but there was one female too smart for Roy. She must have mated frequently with coyotes, as her offspring had tracks twice as large as the ordinary.

Old trappers today will tell you the coyotes in the Needles are still larger than others—the larger type of track is still found consistently over the area—a carryover from that uncaught female.

It was late when Roy asked again where I was going to sleep that night. I told him I was going out into the brush and build a campfire. He invited me to sleep with him in his double sleeping bag. I accepted quickly. I could hear the wind starting to blow in the canyon. The weather was threatening. Roy spread out his bed on a hay mattress. He sat down on one side and took off his shoes, put a plug of chewing tobacco in his mouth and got into bed. I sat down on the other side of the bed, removed my shoes and crawled in alongside him. I slept very well that night. I do not believe that Roy woke up all night to spit out that chewing tobacoo.

Next morning, the first thing Roy did was to sit up in bed and take another large bite of chewing tobacco, put on his shoes and pour a cup of half-warm cowboy coffee. Then, he stirred up the fire and started to prepare breakfast for us—more of that good deer meat, hot sourdough biscuits, jam, and the cowboy coffee. Thanking him gratefully, I went my way with a lighter step, reaching Dugout Ranch early in the afternoon.

In some obvious ways the Needles never matched its initial greeting to me. But from the start I was thrilled with it. There was so much to explore; there were so many places to go.

"Next time I come here, I want to see that—and that." Or perhaps it would be nothing in particular, just the general country. It was the roughest place to hike through that I'd ever seen, because of its many canyons. I've encountered harder ones since, but these were my early complicated challenges. After my first day's entry I don't believe I remembered once again on that trip that the cowboys' tales had lured me there. The sightseeing was awesome, and for each his own first impressions are the most important. Then, too, survival occupied me so intensely that I was aware only of the present. Not until I had been home for some time did I start to put the two together... my childhood listening and my first trip in. Bit by bit, especially with each of my many succeeding hikes, I would recall what John Rohwer and Les Young and the others had told me, as I saw something similar. I found their old tales more and more useful as I came to know the country better.

I would go into Cyclone Canyon, then into Y Canyon and Red Lake Canyon. Taking a new direction I would travel through Elephant Canyon or cross Chesler Park. The Indian pictographs were so numerous I seemed to be forever finding new ones. Many and many a time I would find narrow crevices, just wide enough for passage through, leading to canyons and pockets full of secrets. Once I was exploring the perimeter of Chesler Park, and worked my way sideways through such a crevice for 400 feet. It brought me into a tiny canyon. I came upon a beautiful Kachina doll painting. Near it was a small cave. Inside the cave I found over 200 hand prints on the walls. There were paintings of people carrying large backpacks, with dogs by their sides. Perhaps this was a tale of journeys through the country. I called it the Cave of 200 Hands.

It was strange to realize that I was the first white man to leave my footprint in some of these remote canyons. On one trip I followed Red Lake Canyon down to Cataract Canyon. I camped in a triangle-mouthed cave a hundred feet from Cataract's shore at the first rapids. It turned out to be a smoky place when the wind shifted, and made sleeping out in the cold a pleasure the next night.

On my way back, expecting to go up a familiar canyon, I was puzzled to find myself in an unknown one. I later learned it was part of Twin Canyon, but for me it was the unfamiliar twin. The wrong Twin Canyon was almost a large mistake, as I barely missed stepping into a sinkhole a foot in diameter and about twenty feet deep. It was cone-shaped with the widest part at the bottom. I passed several more of them within a short distance and began to walk very gingerly. It would have been impossible to climb out of one without help. I have since run across similar sinkholes in several other areas in the Needles country.

On the countless visits I have made to Split Rock Cave, I always have noticed the charred bits of the first fire I made there on a cold, wet night. They are still there, although I am the only one who recognizes them. Split Rock looked so dismal then. Little did I think I would be bringing people in for cheery lunches every week years later.

One of my favorite routes became a hike from the 10,000 foot peak of Blue Mountain down into Indian Creek. The change in elevation provides a great variety of vegetation and scenery. Beyond the old Scorup Ranch headquarters at Dugout the canyon drops into desert rock formations as it runs through Cutler sandstone and makes many sharp gooseneck bends. It is full of unusual Indian paintings. One or two scaffold houses remain in caves on the canyon walls. Down near the Colorado River, if a person is lucky, he can find a deer trail to detour around some great falls into the valley below.

On a stiff hike there in cold weather I followed deer trails from canyon to canyon until I came right out over the rims into the Lockhart Basin area. There was a large rock monument which the Indians had piled up centuries ago to mark the head of this trail to the Colorado River. I felt very lucky to have been able to follow their ancient trail all the way. Lockhart Basin is a large escarpment of cliffs with some islands of Wingate out in the middle, a thousand feet lower than the surrounding Wingate cliffs. Displacement of the salt beds below the surface is what may have caused them to drop.

In a side canyon of Hart Canyon, which parallels Lockhart, a wild cow charged me. I picked up a rock to throw, but she caught me off balance and hit my shoulder with her shoulder. Fortunately she knocked me off to the side out of her way, and went running down the canyon. I sat there rather confused. I had never been charged by a cow before in this land where men's tales were of bears and lions. Then I realized that this was a box canyon. She was trapped. Even a cow, when desperate and wild, can be a great hazard. My other dangerous encounter with an animal in the wilderness came many years later in a remote section of the Navajo reservation. As I was approaching a hogan, a Navajo dog ran up and bit me on the leg.

It was easy to see why folks in Monticello would not explore the Needles with me. Life was hard enough for them around town. They saw no reason to go out of their way to add to their concerns. Beauty? Well, wasn't Blue Mountain pretty enough for anyone?

At first I could not get my fill of the Needles. I had taken a long time to make its acquaintance and became so absorbed in it that no other area could draw me. But after a while I remembered that there were many other canyons and mountains waiting.

My first Grand Gulch exploration started in full moonlight. The canyon walls were so beautiful in the strange light, with patches of snow adding to the illumination of the scene, that I went hiking along the bottom of the wash. Snow appeared frequently on my hikes because January often seemed like a good time to go exploring.

In all my hikes I have never found two canyons alike. Each has its own colors, its special erosion features, its own personality. Grand Gulch is a royal canyon of great beauty. Passage down it is easy. It has many springs, superbly beautiful walls, and decorative rimrock that can be admired from the canyon floor. It runs a gamut of different moods for sixty miles—from its head all the way to the San Juan River. There it drops off rapidly in huge waterfalls. Great boulders lie in the water course, and gigantic piles of driftwood line the sides. The final plunge of fifty feet sends the water leaping to the San Juan.

After midnight I forced myself to stop and make camp at a driftwood pile. I found myself—unfortunately—on frozen ground: I never carried bedding and depended on lying on dry ground beside my fire for warmth. My fire was thawing the ground, making it wet. It was a late hour for more work, but I had to move my fire, rake the hot coals and ashes back, then use the warm ground that had been dried by the fire for my bed.

The next day I passed great ice sheets on the shady side of the canyon. The air was crisp and cold. As I hiked over the ice it would crunch and crackle under my feet, echoing from the walls. This made an exciting atmosphere in the stillness of the canyon.

Out in the country alone in the wintertime, a person hears every tiny sound in the extreme stillness as though it were amplified. The land seems to be in the sleep of winter; the least disturbance is greatly noticed.

"This is the place," I said to myself when I reached a narrow pass with a picturesque pinnacle rising from the wall across the way. I could hear water as it trickled down over the slickrock, a beautiful setting for camp.

I explored as many side canyons as possible in the next few days down there. Grand Gulch is rich in prehistoric ruins, dwelling, forts, granaries, cave homes.

It was a place to return to often, and I did. On subsequent visits I surprised myself by finding obscure passageways from the rim that took me all the way to the bottom—although when hiking down there one would think he was locked in by those smooth and often overhanging walls. They were blind exits from inside the canyon. I named one my "secret Indian trail," as broken pieces of pottery and chert chips along the way told me the ancient Indians had also preferred this way of entering.

The rimrocks and upper ledges of Grand Gulch have a special attraction for me. Nature has been tooling and chiseling away at them with great delicacy. Fat boulders rest on slender legs. Caves and hollowed rock abound. It's a pleasant place to camp. From one of my rimrock camps I looked down into the canyon—right down onto a kiva below. Two poles were sticking out of the top. It looked exciting. How could I reach it? I hiked back to one of the Indian trails I knew and traveled down it to the canyon floor. Before long I came to a small structure that looked exactly like the kiva I had spotted from the rim except that the poles were missing. I was confused. But then I thought that my kiva had seemed larger. So I went right on. Much farther down the canyon than I would have supposed, I came upon a hidden entrance to *my* kiva. What a rare discovery it was! I slid down the pole and stood inside. It was splendid, about twenty feet square, a perfectly preserved room floored with about six inches of loose dirt which the rats and chipmunks had dug out of the sand foundation. There was no evidence of digging around the kiva by vandals, but it was empty of artifacts.

Outside again I was musing about the kiva when I saw a nighthawk on the ground. I picked him up to examine him closely; he blinked his eyes and opened his mouth as if yawning. He was not dead at all. I set him back beside his stone. It has been said that these birds hibernate. Here I had found one in its hibernation stage.

Grand Gulch has an arch without a name. It is the biggest and most spectacular of any of the arches along the Grand Gulch drainage. I started calling it Grand Arch and the name stuck.

Another canyon on the maps, named Moqui, began to interest me. When I arrived at its rim to explore it one day I was nursing an extremely sore right eye. A splinter of steel had flown into it while I was sharpening a knife at home at my emory wheel. The weather was bad. Fog lay on all the ridges above me. I climbed a ridge for a good view into the canyon. I had walked a long way through the thick piñon and juniper trees when, to my amazement, I came upon another human track . . . very freshly imprinted in the sand. I stopped sharply on seeing it, to examine it carefully and suspiciously. Then I put my shoe in it. It just fit. I had been walking around in circles up there on that high mesa and could see out of only one eye. I decided that I was lost in a fog and went home. Moqui Canyon represents an unfinished piece of business. I will return to it some day and finish exploring it all the way to Lake Powell.

Perhaps I hadn't been much concerned with the world beyond my map, but the world took an interest in me—along with other young men. The United States went to war. I was like other desert natives: the Navy had more appeal for me than the Army did, so as the Army came closer, I enlisted in the Navy. I thought it might use my abilities as a mechanic.

Service, for me, turned out to be a "Mr. Roberts" affair. I spent the war on a small-craft tender in the South Pacific, doing laundry at night below decks. I was trained as a torpedo technician. I was supposed to keep a World War I torpedo operative on our World War II ship by dismantling the torpedo regularly. It was so outmoded that I doubt it could have hit anything, but it was never fired. Sometimes I wonder how we win wars.

Our ship was a converted freighter, carrying spare parts and equipment to repair subchasers and landing craft. I saw New Guinea and Leyte Gulf from wire-fenced islands, where we were permitted to go once a week from our ship for two cans of beer. That was our leave.

I saved a great deal of money. Gambling didn't lure me. I was paid extra for doing the laundry work, and you can't squander a fortune on two cans of beer a week. Sometimes I envied Alf in the Army, even though he was on the front line in Europe. At least he felt useful. He was using his expert mechanic's ability to repair vehicles brought in at night so they could be driven again the next day.

Since I worked all night I slept and lounged most of the day. I read all the time, everything printed that I could lay my hands on . . . even the Bible, which I went all the way through. Since there wasn't anything else to do I studied for exams and worked up to petty officer second class. The rest of the time I wrote letters home. They were all the same. "I can't stand it on this ship. I'm homesick for my desert canyons. Get me transferred."

The censors must have called my letters to the chaplain's attention, because he came to see me one day. We talked for a while. Finally, when he saw he couldn't change my attitude, he said unsympathetically, "Make up your mind to it. We're all in the same situation." But my letters didn't have to change, and they didn't.

Boredom found its outlet in different forms for different men on board. A first class petty officer decided he had to get rid of a metal locker at the moment the idea occurred to him which was nighttime out at sea. He couldn't get it through the passageway to the deck without cutting it up. With an acetylene torch he went to work on it—near our bunks. Sparks were flying everywhere. A few yards away were stacked 200 torpedo warheads, each weighing 2,000 pounds and solid with TNT. Not one of us said a word. Who cared if we blew up?

Even when the war was over and service points were supposed to be sending men home consecutively, they kept us all rocking there on the Pacific blue. My mother told a friend many years later, "I felt so sorry for Kent. For a year after the war he was still fenced in at the Philippines. He kept writing how they were allowed out only on special privilege weekends. The rest of the time he had to stay inside the fence. I knew how he liked to roam. That was the hardest thing for him—to be fenced in."

At last the great day came. I was on a train in the United States, going home. I wasn't worried about my future. For two years I had been a trained torpedo technician doing laundry below the decks. No civilian work would be as dismal. I would see what came along. Through the years I had been acquiring a variety of useful talents.

What came along was voluntary retirement. I didn't care for farming. I knew I would never return to it. Alf, on the other hand, began planting wheat and beans the week he came home. He really loved it. To my delight, my land at Dodge—originally purchased with the $500 Carnegie prize as down payment and now leased—was offering me a comfortable annual income. It was some of the richest farm land in the county. I was free to roam. And roam I did.

If there were canyons I'd been thinking of while fenced in on the islands, I now went to those canyons. Every time I looked up at Blue Mountain I got excited and went off to climb it . . . green to the top, the pale greens of grasses, the deep sharp greens of trees. Trees along the spines outline the hills and peaks. The sharp slopes have a gentled effect because of the rich growth. Intense shadows flatten out the mountain.

Lore, legend, and memories covered Blue Mountain for me. I visited the shack of my hermit friend. But Old Man West was gone. I inspected the scrap-iron wreckage of the Gold Queen Mine and carted out one of the tramway buckets, which I converted into a camp stove. I recalled the day my uncle brought me to the gold mill across the mountain at Johnson Creek near the Dream Mine. We drove there in a wagon. Walter Lyman showed my uncle how the ore was graded by grinding a sample and panning it out, so that we could see the gold specks in the pan bottom. How fascinating it was for me, a very small boy, to visit a mine so high on a mountain, where men were bustling around horses and wagons and mine equipment. They had started tunneling through West Mountain to bring water to Blanding. The tunnel had gone in just a short distance when mineral traces were discovered in the mountain. So the men dropped the tunnel work and started hunting minerals. They never found any that paid off. But they didn't finish tunneling to bring water to Blanding until after World War II.

In a desultory way I, too, sought the location of Lost Mine, source of so many stories. One said the entrance to the mine was near the rock carving of a six-foot horse, embellished with a moon and a star. Another tale said a sheepherder found an old wheelbarrow at a tunnel starting into a canyon wall. John Young is supposed to have been chasing a wounded mountain sheep over the rims when he came to a place that had the remains of an old tunnel and a kiln for smelting ore. He could never find it again. Another report tells of a man who picked up a rich piece of ore as he passed through the country and, on his deathbed, gave it to his physician with a crude map. There was some truth to it. We actually lent this doctor some horses in the 1930's to go searching for the mine. All the stories revolve around the same general location, Hatch Point, so perhaps there is some truth in them. Perhaps something like a waterfall nearby caused the old mine tunnel to collapse and so disappear.

Sometimes my memory bulges with a collection of unusual sights. It was ten below zero on a January night, when a packrat stood in the firelight of my Indian Creek camp. If there's one animal I won't share my fire with, it's a packrat. I shot him.

That was the week the Colorado River was filled with ice floes. They ground continually along the walls as they moved downstream. Their noise reverberated to the top.

On the rim of Dark Canyon, in the same kind of weather, I found hot air coming up through a crevice that was one inch wide. Green moss was growing around the sides of the opening, with water droplets clinging to the roots. The hot air had to rise a thousand feet through the crevice from the warmer river bottom . . . a canyon ventilating system.

Then, under a ledge in a different canyon, near Alkali Ridge, I found—prehistoric firepits with glazed sand! Now how did those ancient people get a fire going hot enough to produce that?

Back in the canyon country I discovered a rock ladder carved by the ancients. Climbing the toeholds in the rock put me on top of the mesa at Davis Canyon. I had never suspected there was any place of exit in Davis, as its walls are high and sheer. Hiking around the mesa I looked down into Horse Canyon for a beautiful view of Castle Arch. A second look showed me another tremendous arch, closer to the bottom of the canyon. I climbed down and found it. Later, while guiding the National Park Service into the area, I showed them the arch which they named "The Fortress."

Salt Creek is a place by itself. I can imagine the pleasure of the early cowboys when they rode up that small side canyon, now called Angel Canyon and saw the lovely Angel high on the skyline. They must have seen it. And yet, it's funny about the Angel. There were no cowboy comments about her. And although there were guided horse parties down Salt Creek in the '30's, none of them ever visited Angel Arch. Either she was not known or she did not stir up much interest. So although I had heard about the arch from a few prospectors, I did not bother to visit it until my brother, Melvin, piloted me over the Needles. When I saw that arch from the air I knew it was the Angel, and I knew she was worth an introduction.

On my next hike down Salt Creek I turned in eagerly to explore her special side canyon. She is a wonder—ninety feet high, with folded wings, a long gown, a cherub's face, and her own stone gateway to the sky arching behind her. I've seen her 800 times since and she is still a wonder to me.

Perhaps the cowboys used to climb into a cave in upper Salt Creek to see the flamboyant red, white, and blue life-sized painting of a man. Nearby is a wall of beautiful death-mask paintings. No vehicle can travel into upper Salt Creek.

On my first hike all the way down Salt Creek from its head at Cathedral Butte it was remarkable to come to Kirk's cabin, once a pioneer ranch, with Kirk's scythe still fastened to the remains of the walls and some of his cooking utensils still hanging about the fireplace, now with the sky for a roof. Kirk had set his doorway facing directly towards an arch across the canyon, called Kirk's Arch by the cowboys.

After visiting Angel Arch and Castle Arch many times via the canyon floors (it takes over two days of hiking time to go from one to the other), I discovered on the mesa above that they are only about a mile apart. I could go from one to the other in a half hour.

I became the local gunsmith. Craftsmanship of every kind appealed to me. By now I had a varied collection surrounding that first Springfield rifle from Chester. I enjoyed rebuilding them, and made quite a few military rifles into sporting guns by changing the sights, removing extra metal and wood to lighten the weight, or by building a sportier stock. I found that converted military rifles take more punishment, are sturdier, and are more dependable to use in the field. I myself rarely went anywhere without a gun. I was almost always alone in an empty land.

My canyon map expanded again when I started exploring west of the Colorado. There was a whole new world over there. I was camping for the first time at the San Rafael Reef when I met a stockman who asked, "Seen any bears?"

"No," I answered. "I've never seen a bear. I don't suppose there are any left here any more."

"Not like Swazey's bear," he said, and started laughing. Then he told me that many years ago the Swazey men and their friends were known for being rugged. A party of them came riding up to their summer cabin in the area.

One went in and hollered, "There's a bear in here." There was a live bear in there.

They were all great men for a joke. Swazey and company slammed the door and locked it, leaving their pal inside. He had to pick up a camp stool and fight it out. He killed the bear. That inspired me to search for Swazey's cabin while I was over on the west side of the river. I didn't find it, but I located Horseshoe Canyon and its giant mural. It is a great panel of prehistoric Indian paintings, done mainly in bright red on a wall of smooth beige sandstone. The figures are splendidly costumed. One of them is ten feet tall. The wall is a hundred feet long, and there are enough figures to fill it.

I also returned to river running with Nevills and realized the peak of my boatman's ambition. I ran Grand Canyon.

I felt a great thrill as we left Lee's Ferry and passed under the high bridge at Marble Canyon. I was tense but glad I had so much good river experience to support me.

Norm followed the technique established by Major

Norm Nevills and Kent running the rapids.

Powell long ago. Arriving at the head of a rapids, we pulled ashore and went down the beach to study it. The "looking over" decision is final. Once you are on the way the action is swift, and you cannot see the problems as well as you can when studying them quietly from shore. If, however, you are not able to put the boat in the place you figured on, then you must just do the best you can to avoid boulders or waves that might upset you. Frequently there is nothing you can do about a problem except wait and watch to see what happens. As Norm said often, "The main idea is to avoid hitting rocks."

At our very first rapids, Badger Creek, Norm decided in favor of fast maneuvering, which meant leaving the passengers on shore to walk around. We did it again at the next, Soap Creek Rapids. The briefings were always helpful: "Go around on the right-hand side of that rock. Pull hard on your oars as you approach it."

Things were going smoothly and I relaxed, but I did not give up my fears of Sockdolager and Grapevine Rapids, because no one could walk around them. Their sheer cliffs come straight down to the water. When we reached them, however, they did not seem so threatening, and all the boats went floating through.

We generally wanted to run down the "tongue" of a rapids. If there were big holes we would have to "slip off" from the hole. A hole is the area downstream from a big boulder, with a waterfall washing over the rock, building into a reverse wave on the downstream edge of the hole. Boats can be tipped over by this turbulent water or by the backlash of the waves. It requires some fast maneuvering to avoid this. With passengers on board, the boat is heavier. Therefore it's harder to change course. High water makes an easier run because many of the rocks are adequately submerged. Every rapids is different. Sometimes the passengers rode through and sometimes they walked around.

When we reached the Little Colorado River, we found a large rattlesnake lying on the banks.

"Kent, do you think a rattler can strike if it's hanging by its tail?" one of our party asked.

"I've never been told," I said, keeping the snake pinned on the ground with a forked stick.

"Well, of course, don't do it if it's dangerous, but it would be remarkable to get a picture of someone holding one upside down."

"Is your camera ready?" I had suddenly decided. "Here you are. Hurry up." And I suspended the rattler by his tail at arm's length while they photographed it. Though I thought the pictures were fine when I saw them later (one was even published in a magazine) I would not repeat that research.

The water in the Little Colorado is bright blue. We could see the bottom in six feet of water. Its contrast with the muddy Colorado was the subject of many a photograph.

Phantom Ranch is the halfway mark. I had heard about it for years, of course: the resort at the bottom of Grand Canyon.

"Do you think," I asked a passenger, "that all this luxury is too fancy for us campers?" The Ranch has fine cabins, a dining room, and a swimming pool, all deep down, a mile down, below the rims. We had a two-day layover at Phantom Ranch while we restocked the boats and took on a few new people. Some of our first passengers were leaving us. They had a choice of two ways to get up to the rims and the world above—by a strenuous hike on the trails up the walls or by riding a mule up the trails. The same two choices were offered to those coming down to join us.

I still remember Horn Creek Rapids, after we shoved off again, with its water swirling around the granite ledge, making a tremendous eddy and holes in the river current. The whirlpools in the Grand Canyon are a challenge; but I never thought of them as desperate, because even if they pulled a boat under they would have to release it very soon; then it could float down below the rapids. The passengers could catch and hold on to the boat.

I was always glad to see those big bad ones get behind me though. Some rapids produced waves so big I was expecting the boat to drop out of sight, but it never did.

Not all the moments were tense ones. There were long light-hearted stretches. One of the delights of a July river trip is Nature's handy cooling system. Everyone soaks in the river and can remain cool while sitting wet in the blazing sun. Twenty minutes later each is ready for another dip.

We stopped at beautiful Deer Creek Falls, with its large, clear stream making a seventy-five foot drop into the Colorado. We fished at cold Tapeats Creek and got enough trout for dinner.

We passed the mouth of Kanab Canyon and camped at gorgeous Havasu. A narrow canyon entrance opened into clear blue waters. Although it was a place of great beauty, there was very little sleeping space for bedrolls. I chose a narrow ledge, three feet wide, with a sheer drop of thirty feet on the outside. I was cautious about sneezing or turning over during the night.

At Havasu, Norm and I climbed to the rim of the inner gorge and were jumping across where the walls narrowed. It was thirty feet down to the water of Havasu Creek. Along came two members of our party, a father and son. They were speculating on the possibility of the boy's jumping down this narrow crooked crevice to the water. The creek water was at best four feet deep.

Finally the young fellow said, "I believe I can make it."

"Well, all right," answered his father, "but be sure to pull back your head when you go past that ledge about halfway down." The boy poised on the rim and jumped. He managed to pull back his head as he went past the ledge, feet first, and landed with a big splash.

Looking up, he said, "See, I made it all right." He seemed satisfied with the one jump and did not repeat it. Perhaps landing in such shallow water jarred him quite a bit.

Norm had arranged for another of his imaginative experiments at Lava Falls. We were met by Mr. Riffey, the ranger of Grand Canyon National Monument. He delivered the mail! Those who were preadvised had made use of this remote address and had envelopes delivered to them in the heart of Grand Canyon. Mr. Riffey stayed overnight with us. We returned him to his shore in the morning, and he started up his six-hour ascent as we lined our boats down the side of Lava Falls. It is one of the worst rapids in Grand Canyon.

We arrived at Lake Mead with a party of happy passengers. But one of the boatmen was happier than the rest. The Grand run had been even more thrilling and beautiful than I could ever have imagined it so many years before, when I had my first chance to look in over the rim after a San Juan trip.

PART 2
The Dwindling Wilderness

CHAPTER 15

The one thing I couldn't find in the canyons was my life's companion. I had to go to Arizona for her. The town of Mesa introduced me to pretty, blonde Fern.

We met when we were both vacationing there. I knew she was the one, and she was attracted to me, but her father wasn't ready to give her up. Three days after I began visiting her, he pointed his finger at me and said, "Young man, you'd better go home and let this girl think over your relationship so you will not rush her." I sensed that he did not appreciate my presence and association with Fern, so I drove home to Monticello and corresponded with her.

Fern lived on a farm at Draper, near Salt Lake City, with her mother, father, brother, and sister. They worked hard, raising fruit, tomatoes, hay, and grain, and it was up to her to help her father and brother on the farm. She and her mother and sister took care of 3,000 laying chickens. When her brother was called into the service he turned over to Fern the additional care of seven cows he had been milking. Her parents went away for a few days, leaving Fern and her sister to run the farm. A local man came by at that time and offered Fern a price for the cows. She sold them instantly. Her dad was surprised when he returned, but had never liked to milk them. How could he ever part with such an enterprising helper?

It happened that my Uncle Mons, who was perhaps 50, was going to marry a young woman in Mesa early in May. I wrote Fern, asking if I could come and see her again. With her own and her father's approval, I returned to Mesa with Mons. I was very much surprised that her father seemed to think better of me. On May 9, 1949, he said, "How would you and Fern like to go over to New Mexico and get married today?" We were both astonished, but decided that if he was in the mood for our getting married, that was the time.

Fern and I and her parents and mine, who were also there for Mons' wedding, drove 150 miles to Lordsberg, New Mexico, to be married by the Justice of the Peace. We drove back to Mesa and remained there for two weeks, then took her folks to their home at Draper, Utah. Fern's friends and relatives held festive wedding receptions for us at Draper. Finally we left for Monticello on our own, set up housekeeping for ourselves, and embarked on a year's honeymoon.

I was broke at the time. My only property was a Model A Ford and the same dog, Skippy, but what I wanted most to do was introduce Fern to my canyon country. Twelve months later we were ready to admit that the introduction was rather a complete one. We camped out all the time and roamed the mountains, mesas, and canyons, coming to town only to replenish supplies.

One of our first trips, of course, was into the Needles. That year the road had been bulldozed up Elephant Hill. So, although the hill was extremely steep, we were able to drive the Model A up its east side and leave it at the top. In later years, when the dirt had been washed away, only a four-wheel-drive vehicle could manage it. Then we hiked in from Elephant Hill.

We stayed mainly in the high mountain country during the summer. In the La Sal mountains we drove up Geyser Pass and made a long camp there. One day Skippy and I climbed all five peaks in the center section of the La Sals, including my old favorite, Mt. Peale, which is over 12,721 feet. We returned to camp after dark, both of us tired and hungry. Even Skippy was lagging far behind. But things were different now. There was lovely Fern, waiting, with dinner ready.

I wanted to show Fern the beautiful cliff dwellings in Grand Gulch. We camped near the roundup corral at the edge of the canyon so that we could hike in early in the morning. The masonry and pottery of the Grand Gulch prehistoric people is very fine. I knew that Fern would want to see as much of it as she could. We climbed around the canyon ledges to look in on each one. In my eagerness to lead her to a wall with fingerprints still visible in the ancient mortar, my heel caught on a rock, I tripped, and was almost thrown over the two-foot ledge for a 100-foot drop. I teetered sickeningly before regaining my balance. That was the closest I have ever come to a bad fall.

Fern was extremely tired on the way back and didn't think she could make it. I made a harness out of a long rope, to go around Skippy's shoulders. As I encouraged Skippy to follow me, he pulled Fern right up over those steep ledges. It was such a good idea that whenever she wore out on any hike from then on, we would harness up Skippy and he would tow her out. He pulled her from Bear's Ears to Long Point, and in and out of many spots in the Needles.

We would practice shooting with my various guns. Fern became proficient. A few years ago she won a shooting match in competition with some hunting experts; I recalled her practising in the canyons, as she used the same technique at the match. She sat calmly on the ground, raised her high-powered rifle toward the target, took slow aim, fired her three shots, and gathered her prizes.

When another fall rolled around, I got a job harvesting

wheat for my brother-in-law. The uranium boom was just hitting the county. We moved ten miles south of Monticello to my parents' unoccupied Blue Mountain Ranch, to operate it as a guest ranch for prospectors and mill processors. It expanded in all sorts of ways. Deer hunters came in the fall, lived at the ranch, and hired me for their guide. From fifteen to thirty hunters would arrive from California and all go home with their bags; deer were that plentiful. Vacationers came in the summer. I would take them for a day's scenic trip.

I always believed the ranch should open on April 1. Fern and I were there for opening day and never left it untended until we closed on October 30. It was a demanding occupation. Fern's mother and my partner's wife ran the kitchen. Fern's father and my partner helped me as handymen. Fern marketed, kept books, cleaned cabins, drove, and did all the other unassigned jobs.

Our vacationers liked to ride. That meant maintaining horses, and the horse was always my least favorite animal. Horses continued to make trouble for me, especially an old packhorse named Black Jack. I was leading Black Jack by a rope one morning to take out a group of hunters. He got the lead rope wound around a tree by taking the opposite side from me. He jumped when the rope tightened. The cinch strap broke. I landed on my back with my gun barrel pushed so deeply in the mud that it was standing up next to me by itself. I almost had my head kicked in, but I guess I was lucky: his hoof just grazed my hair. Another time, I was riding Black Jack through two feet of snow near Cold Spring when I saw a large deer just ahead of me. I dismounted to shoot. As the rifle shot rang, the horse took off. He ran right back to the ranch, leaving me to wade through two feet of snow for three miles. I was wishing I had shot the horse instead of the deer.

After we closed the ranch each season we spent the winter at Mesa, Arizona. I had my eye on an emerald green Jeep that was sitting in the used-car lot in Mesa. At the right price, I bought it. "Emmy" met the canyonlands the following spring. Now we had a vehicle that would take us over the merest trace of a road, and often no road at all. That year Fern got her first experience driving Jeeps. Emmy moved us from the exploration into the organization period. We used Emmy for uranium prospecting and for guiding the deer hunters, the Senior Explorers Scouts, and the Utah Fish and Game Commission on trips into the Needles. We helped the Forest Service and the BLM with transportation into Beef Basin and other places. When our ranch vacationers heard my descriptions of the hard-to-reach country, they began to ask to go there. We didn't charge for that. If anyone showed an interest I was glad to take him.

A group of us local people went off to find the old Mormon Trail of 1880. While those pioneers could cross the Land of Rock and Sand with their wagons, we could not do the same with motor vehicles until 1958, when a uranium company spent $38,000 for a road from Lake Canyon to Slick Rock Hill. The group lost the trail after it left Grey Mesa. I walked ahead of the Jeeps, thinking, "If the old wagon tracks had crushed the brush, then for years after the livestock would follow the easiest path and keep the old trail alive." I picked up the livestock trail and it led right to the place that Ed Lyman recognized as the Chutes . . . a landmark of that old pioneer trail.

Our group was retracing a historic venture. We reestablished the route of 1880. How we marveled to think that 250 people with wagons had struggled through this wild terrain seventy years earlier. Men, women, and children crossed 220 miles of rock upheaval, hewing trails out of solid stone. A baby was born in a blizzard on the way. They froze, starved, strained—and made it, without a loss. They had gathered from areas near Salt Lake City to cross the Colorado River and establish the place they called Bluff.

Our exploring group had the advantage of seeing all the remains and ruins of that original pioneer trip: an old wagon, pieces of broken glass and china on the rocks and in the sand, hub spokes, wheels. We left everything untouched. But the public treatment of that trail, once we announced it, taught me a sad lesson about souvenir hunters. All relics disappeared within a few years.

Fern and I eventually put 75,000 miles on the Jeep. In spite of all the use we made of Emmy, I was able to keep her so tuned up that ten years later we sold her for our purchase price. Emmy was still worth it.

When Norm Nevills died in a plane crash in 1949, the news flashed around San Juan County by word of mouth quicker than papers could print it . . . he had become an institution. I received the sad news from someone on the street.

Frank Wright took over the river trips. I worked for Frank occasionally. Fern and I would help transport the passengers' automobiles from place to place or help pick up boating parties at Lee's Ferry. Sometimes I also served as boatman. It would generally be arranged at a time when Fern could accompany the party as a passenger.

Fern's first river trip was a spontaneous eruption that bubbled up out of a good-natured offer and carried her with it down the San Juan River. Fern had come to Mexican Hat to see us off. The two women passengers started urging her to come along.

"It's time you tried the rivers, too, Fern," said one. "Come on, it's going to be a good trip."

"I couldn't," she answered. "I didn't bring anything with me for a trip."

"We'll share our things!" They were gleeful as they threw open their cases and started pulling out clothes and tossing them to Fern on shore. She caught them, but still demurred.

"Thanks very much. I appreciate your wanting me," she said calmly, "but I guess I won't."

"No, we won't take them back. You're to wear them on this ride."

She stood there on the bank, holding the garments. We were ready to leave. Then, just as calmly as she had refused, she said, "By heck, I will."

We delayed our departure while she went behind a

bush and changed. I hardly recognized her when she stepped out in her borrowed finery: the new wardrobe was partly too large, partly too small for her; the bright red culottes and green- and orange-striped shirt were never meant by the designers to be worn together. One of the men clapped an extra hat of his on her head, and we were off. Her borrowed wardrobe caused her no concern. We were always flexible in our ways and ready to accept what came along. With a start like this, the trip had to be hilarious. Everyone teased Fern about her outfit.

"Come along, orphan," they would call, or "Let the orphan go first," as the men made way for her across a ledge on a hike.

There was something about the way that Fern looked all day every day in those culottes that made me say to her, "Never wear culottes again."

By then I had run all of the Green River and all of the Colorado River, from Wyoming to Lake Mead, except Cataract Canyon. Most naturally I wanted to close the gap in the record, but I also simply wanted to get acquainted with Cataract, which had a reputation for being worse in some ways than Grand Canyon.

Before Frank had purchased the Nevills' operation I had contemplated organizing commercial river trips. With that in mind I had purchased three large rubber army-surplus rafts. It was with some relief that I heard of Frank's plans, as I had not genuinely wanted the worry of operating river trips. It was hard enough being a boatman. But I still owned the rafts.

Fern and I tried one for a trip of our own through Grey and Desolation Canyons, from Jensen to Green River. It was a peaceful run and no test of what the rafts could do. I still didn't know what the rafts' capabilities were when I may have said to Alf, "I'm curious about Cataract Canyon, and I want to run it on one of my rafts. Do you want to go with me?"

Or perhaps he suggested it to me, knowing that I had the equipment. At any rate, we set out together to run Cataract. Alf was already a big farmer in the community. But he was still a good partner in exploring. He would have made a fine wilderness man if he hadn't been everlastingly tied up in his farming.

We were both toughened up from a summer's work when we launched from Moab on September 1.

That was the most vigorous steady-action non-stop river trip ever taken. We were full of nervous energy, and so we rowed. We just rowed and rowed and came plowing down through the canyons.

Arriving at Cataract Canyon's first rapids, we studied the passage. I was going to line it. I wasn't used to rubber rafts. Alf said, "Let's run it."

"All right," I agreed, "if you stay on shore." I was accustomed to practicing the care necessary for wooden boats. It is vital to be particular with them. If they hit rocks, their sides get bashed in.

I soon discovered that it makes little difference what happens to those rubber rafts. In fact, in a later rapids, we rode right up on top of a big boulder and stuck there until Alf jumped off casually, gave us a push, and jumped on again. Such lack of planning would be unthinkable in the wood rowboats; planning is part of what makes the trip with wooden craft a more sporting and greater adventure.

When I joined Alf on shore after running the first rapids, we made camp. "It looks safe enough," he said. "I'll run the rest with you." Ruell would have enjoyed our supper that night. It was our most reliable river menu, catfish—with a new characteristic added. All the catfish we caught in Cataract Canyon were white. We had never seen white catfish elsewhere, nor have we heard anyone else mention white catfish. But we weren't color blind, we couldn't have been dreaming for four days, and we caught white catfish daily. One afternoon those fish were really boisterous: we could see dozens of them surfacing in the waters ahead of us, gleaning their food.

We ran every single rapids and stopped to look over only two or three of the bad ones. We would not, however, want anyone to think lightly of the hazards of

Cataract Canyon. It is a big, powerful stretch. Even to an experienced river man, as I was by then, it was impressive. From the start of the canyon the rapids follow one another so closely that there is rarely time between rapids to think and plan. That problem gives the canyon its bad reputation. Our advantage was that we were running at low water. Harder work. Less danger.

At Dark Canyon there are three consecutive rapids and three places where the boulders are extremely obtrusive and close together. We lined up so perfectly with the first one that the river carried us right between the three bad spots, with just exactly room for the raft to slide by.

We had been rowing like mad and continued to do so, rather than just sit, although Dark Canyon ends the rough water. We came tearing into Hite five days after leaving Moab.

Cataract was a river canyon that Fern preferred hearing about to trying. After her happy float down the San Juan and Grey and Desolation Canyons, she went through Glen Canyon and, finally, Grand. When she wasn't on a trip she would meet me at the debarkation point and come home with the river party.

The year following my trip with Alf through Cataract Canyon was the year Frank Wright ran a trip from Green River, Utah, to Lake Mead. This meant Grand Canyon again, and I welcomed it. I was no longer tense. You always feel confident once you've had an experience.

One member of our party, Russ Anspach, had a tiny yellow rubber raft with an outboard motor which he enjoyed running independently with us, even in Cataract Canyon. In the Cataract rapids he used oars to control his raft. On the second day he hit a large wave that flung him upside down. Russ clung to the side, swirling through the rocks, until one of our boats could come to his rescue. Undismayed, he returned to his raft and continued to follow us through Cataract on that little yellow float.

After a successful run through the wild Dark Canyon

rapids we reached the quiet river. Frank dug a three-horse-power motor out of his hold and attached it to the yellow raft. We tied the four big cataract boats in a string, and Russ towed all of us to Hite twice as fast as we could row. The boatmen no longer had anything to do —a spoiling situation for all that muscle. We wound up having water fights with the passengers and pushing each other into the river.

Fern was waiting to join us at Hite for her first meeting with Glen Canyon. This time she had her own wardrobe. She was going all the way through Grand Canyon with us to Lake Mead. She was especially worried about Sockdolager and Grapevine Rapids, which made me wonder if I had conveyed to her my earlier uneasiness over those same places. We had no trouble running them, but I was generally surprised throughout the trip at how different the river was. It was six years since I had made my first trip through Grand Canyon with Norm. This was my second Grand run. A different water stage made some of the rapids hardly recognizable. It was hard to associate them with the previous trip.

At Hermit Falls, famous for its large waves, I was following the leader when a lateral wave hit my boat at the head of the rapids and shoved it right out into the middle of the river, where the waves looked mountainous.

"Hang on!" I called to Fern, who happened to be my only passenger that day, and we went riding down the center of the river through the largest waves I've ever been over in a cataract boat. It was the most exciting ride I've ever had on any river. Frank was cross; he thought I'd done it on purpose. But once the lateral wave struck me unexpectedly, it would have been just wasted effort to try to get back to calmer water. There wasn't anything I could do but ride.

At Upset Rapids the youngest boatman plowed into a reverse wave and I watched his boat flip over. One of the passengers could not swim. She was lost to view for a few seconds because she came up under the boat which was upside down. She clung to the boat's rope, however, and had air to breathe in there while the current swept her below the rapids. I hurried to get her to shallow water. All was well. But I was reminded that a boatman has to be alert every second in fast water. There are many hidden dangers waiting for him, and he can never afford to relax his vigilance or become overconfident.

As we righted the boat a carton of eggs fell in the river. Eggs sink, we found out, and got busy retrieving as many as we could by feeling around the bottom with our feet. Hunger won out with me; for every two eggs I retrieved for the boat, I swallowed the contents of one raw.

At Tanner's Mine another boatman and I found a case of dynamite, labeled 1932. The thing you want to know about a 1932 product in 1953 is, is it still good? We carried it out to the river's edge and set it on a large boulder. All stood back, ears covered, as I took aim with my high-powered rifle. It was just fine . . . a ball of fire, followed by smoke, a concussion wave, and a big bang. After seeing the ball of fire you feel the air "whshhhh" against you, then you hear the concussion. The sound echoed and re-echoed from Grand Canyon's walls.

At Lake Mead, the end of our trip, I was surprised at how far the silt had extended up the lake in the six years since my first trip. It was approximately thirty miles farther up from the entry into Lake Mead than it had been six years before. The lake was actually filling up . . . and fast. Large islands and banks of sand had choked it up thirty miles from the head; the dying river currents were able to cut only a few feeble channels through the silt bars.

CHAPTER 16

On the Cataract trip, as we passed Spanish Bottom, I pointed out the pink and white spires high above on the rim to a passenger, Mary Beckwith. Their unusual formation entranced her. I told her there were many more of them in the Needles.

"How can you get in to see them?" she asked.

"I have a Jeep. I'll take you in there."

"Could you get more Jeeps? Other people might want to go."

Yes, I thought I could get more.

"When can we go in?" she asked.

"This Fall."

The group discussed it many times on the way down the river. I shaped it into a plan as they asked me questions. I had always had an idea I'd like to conduct guided tours. Becky—as Mary Beckwith was called—sparked the idea.

That was my first paying guided Jeep trip. It was also

the Needles' first commercial Jeep trip. Emmy was responsible for it all. Mary Beckwith organized it. Seven travelers met us at the ranch in the fall: Mary Beckwith, Dr. Bill Thompson, Joe Dudziak, Joseph Muench, a photographer, Frank Wright, Paul Wright, and two girls named Naomi and Roz. They were all filled with explorers' anticipation. Each brought his own sleeping bag. Frank, Fern, and I were the drivers.

I had some worries, but it was fun leading others to the beauty and wonder that had been ours alone. I tried some new places but mainly took them where I'd been before. As I had expected, the allure of the Needles caught them in its grip as firmly as it had the prehistoric Indians, the cowboys, and me. "What a rock tangle," they said. We visited pictographs and petroglyphs, camped beside pink and white sculptured pinnacles, gazed down at the confluence of the rivers, and marveled at the mysteries of nature. They gave up trying to figure out what direction they were facing. It was hunting season, so I shot a deer for several nights' feasts.

"Kent," called Becky on an afternoon hike. "See what I've found." She emerged from a small cave holding up a brilliant feather piece, possibly a chin mask. It is now in our Monticello museum. There was nothing else in the cave but some bits of charcoal and a few pottery chips. We have never found anything else like the mask.

A story that appeared in *Natural History* magazine about us brought a few inquiries. That gave me the idea of writing to Randall Henderson, founder and publisher of *Desert Magazine.* He was the authority on the desert Southwest. I told him that I thought I would be a qualified guide, having had a great deal of wilderness experience as well as mechanic's training with vehicles. My idea was to take him into the Land of Standing Rocks, west of the Colorado River, as well as into the Needles.

Standing Rocks is a valley below the Orange Cliffs. Solitary purple stone monoliths rise high on the valley floor in a majestic, single-file parade. There had been a cowboy's horse trail over the Wingate ledge of the

Orange Cliffs. But a prospector's bulldozer had just made it possible for Jeeps to pass along the old path that is called Flint Trail.

Fern and I had gone over there several times in the preceding years to hike down and explore it. Now, since we were Jeep owners, we tried driving it. With expansion had come the purchase of a second Jeep. We worked out our Jeep route through Standing Rocks, finally leaving via Squaw Trail to the top of Land's End.

At my invitation Randall Henderson came out, took the trip, and wrote a beautiful story about us and Standing Rocks. With him came Dr. Bill Thompson, Joe Dudziak, Becky, and Dr. Mel Hurley. To my great delight, the trip went smoothly. Although I had been there several times before, the wilderness was still roadless. I had to make my own trails as I led a trusting group to corners I had not yet explored. I also had to avoid wasting valuable time getting hung up on dead ends and having to backtrack.

We now took two vehicles into Standing Rocks, with Frank Wright driving one. The old road out of Green River to Hanksville was still a challenge of its own at that time. We came to the San Rafael River and stopped. Randall Henderson and I walked out on the bridge's framework. We rearranged its loose planks by hand to fit the wheel span of our Jeeps. The next vehicle coming by would have to reset them for itself.

It had snowed during the night but the day was sunny and clear. Everyone was excited as we crossed Antelope Flats and started working our way into the Robbers' Roost country. When we reached the top of Flint Trail the sun was dropping low behind us.

The trail top is a high vantage point. We gazed for a long time at the vast land of rainbow rock confusion below us. We saw ragged escarpments in the distance. Far across the Colorado, to our east, the Needles country was backed by shadowy mountains. The wind-and-rain-carved pinnacles were calling us from down below. We piled into the Jeeps and started down Flint Trail. Nobody flinched—not even when I had to stop and back up on two hairpin turns, or when I had to stop again to push boulders out of our path.

We camped in a piney corner at the trail's foot. Beyond our camp I found some dynamite left by prospectors. There is only one thing to do with dynamite, and I had become an expert at it. It went up in a tremendous explosion when I fired into it.

Two mules, left by sheepherders, were so glad to see people that they kept approaching our second camp, snorting, running away, then approaching again. Fern found a large arrow with a hole through the center, the only pierced arrowhead I have ever seen.

"Where to this morning, Kent?" each person asked as he tied up his bedroll and dumped it on the Jeep.

"Let's go see the Spanish Stairs."

"What are they?"

Becky looked wise. "That's the trail up here from Spanish Bottom. That's where this trip began."

We hiked single file through cactus and primrose while I told them the snatch of known history. The crossing of the Colorado down below to Red Lake Canyon on the other side may have been a winter route for the early Spanish traders between Santa Fe and northern California. The horse trail down the 1,500-foot wall to Spanish Bottom had been built into stairs to bridge difficult ledges. If the Spaniards constructed this stairway they must have used Indian slave labor, since some of the rocks weigh a thousand pounds.

Spanish Bottom is a square mile of beautiful shore, with cottonwood trees on the banks and a green valley. In a canyon near Ferron, about 70 miles away, seven Spanish crosses carved into an overhang seem to bear out the legend of the trail. We went down the trail far enough to see the massive old construction.

At the head of the stairs were the pinnacles that had caught Becky's attention on the Cataract Canyon river trip. They corresponded with the rock formation in the Needles. Randall Henderson named their arrangement Doll House.

Our Jeeps purred and moaned their way over and

around shimmering rock dunes the second day, as I was anxiously watching for a good cave. Heavy clouds were already gathering, with the promise of a wet night. It would be good to plan ahead for a dry camp. I found a second horse trail but not a cave. All those beautiful billowing hills curved smoothly outward. The new horse trail took us through Sunrise Valley to Lizard Rock. On the way we spotted a large arch which we planned to examine the following day.

Each of us was finding some feature of the area that had special appeal for him. I was thinking, "This area is more open and more enclosed than the Needles." What I meant was that the valley was wider but that the walls surrounding it were much higher.

Everyone gloried in the Standing Rocks themselves. Sculptured from dark red Cutler rock, they are hundreds of feet high. One is shaped like a candlestick, one like a totem pole. Lizard Rock is the largest . . . and as we climbed them, photographed them, lunched in their shade, I found our cave in the base of one. Full of inward relief, my worries for the night gone, I, too, was now able to enjoy the Standing Rocks.

I had been right about the weather. It rained hard that night but we were all snug and dry in Kent's Cave. By the time we were ready to explore again the next morning, the sun was shining. On this trip Fern and I developed our technique of driving parallel, never letting one Jeep follow in the path of the other, to avoid setting up established tracks. Also, to lighten the Jeeps' loads, I cached gas and food supplies on the way in, then picked them up again on the way out.

We went first to the new arch. Some climbed on top of it. Others photographed it. We unanimously agreed to name it Henderson Arch, in tribute to the man who was spreading his appreciation of desert trails to so many others.

At our first campfire Randall Henderson taught me his "burn, bang, and bury" technique of disposing of rubbish. I had always tried scrupulously to leave clean camps, which frequently meant I was carrying back to

Monticello all the empty cans we had used on our trips. Burning them erases the food odor, so that animals will not dig them up again; flattening them makes them more compact; and burying them means deeper than three or four inches. Now, with the increase in traffic to these areas, I am back to our earlier method. The Park Bureau's request states, "If you can carry it in, you can carry it out." That is what we all do today.

CHAPTER 17

Just as one customer recommends another, one press or magazine article leads to another. It began to seem as though the world were coming to our door. We guided visitors from every corner of the United States. Then people started arriving from England, France, India, Japan, Australia, and many other distant parts of the world. Many of them returned again and again to become our firm, personal friends. All appreciated the enchantment of the land.

Our long list included magicians and mechanics, actors and accountants, secretaries and senators, writers and printers, engineers and educators, photographers and farmers, doctors and dancers, executives and clerks. All were philosophers and many became poets, at least momentarily inspired by the great and unusual land. One of our passengers came out for her first trip when she was 80. She got along better than some of her younger companions and was the first to carry her sleeping bag, rolled up and tied, to the Jeep each morning.

"Now, Mabel," Fern admonished her, when she returned two years later for another trip, "you let those men carry your sleeping bag for you. Don't let me hear you did it."

Our correspondence increased. Our parties increased. Each year found us ordering more supplies, buying more gas, more sleeping bags, adding air mattresses. We acquired more vehicles and started a branch operation in Moab. We were getting a modern gloss, but I clung to my Dutch oven cookery over hot coals. My lonely winter camps had ingrained in me a kind of culinary procedure I could never change. To my amazement, many an editor who traveled with us devoted more of his report to my special way of raking a fire and cooking on the coals than to the scenery he was privileged to see.

We soon learned that there was more to operating a guide service than taking people safely and happily into the wilderness. We studied licensing, insurance, bookkeeping. It was necessary to become active members of the city Chamber of Commerce and the county tourist bureau. We cooperated with allied services—river runners, pilots of airplane services. We took Utah state travel shows to Texas and California and Illinois.

As time went by, through constant practice, we developed considerable competence at appearing before official state hearing boards at Salt Lake City. We found our exclusive guide privilege challenged often by those to whom we had made it look easy and attractive. Occasionally one of them knew a little about following us into the lonesome places. With barely enough visitors to occupy one service like ours, we defended our priority staunchly. Financially, our operation was only marginally successful. Many years we felt lucky to break even, by the time we had paid extra drivers, purchased new equipment, and paid our other operational expenses. But we were enjoying it.

Many of the problems were new. When a business starts growing around you, instead of your stepping into an established one in which someone can instruct you, the decisions are endless. But it seems that a person can figure out just about anything and come up with the right answer if he is not pressured or distracted. Whether the problem is mechanical—a breakdown or flat tire in a lost land—or operational, or human, I can solve it if allowed to sit down quietly and concentrate on it. My first punctured tire on a trip called for a patching job. I asked the woman of the party to brew a cup of tea for us all while I worked. By the time she had the tea ready, I had the tire ready.

From the first suggestion of the creation of a park out of the canyonlands, Fern and I worked ardently for it. We helped entertain senators, governors, cabinet members, and reporters, as they came to visit the Needles and consider its value. We testified for a park at hearings held locally. We spoke in favor of it at all opportunities. We thought the park would be good for the country and the county.

At one hearing Fern spoke so positively that a daily paper reported, " ... there is only one person in San Juan County who knows what he wants as far as the national park is concerned, and that is Fern Frost."

Another metropolitan daily quoted her remarks at a later congressional hearing: " 'The land in the Needles,' said Fern Frost, 'will support only one cow per thousand acres, and that's for only part of the year. The park ought to be worth more than that.' "

Just as I had learned tracking and trail use from the cowboys of my childhood, and as I had learned to think about a greater range of subjects from Doris Nevills' encouragement, the search for knowledge, once begun, continued at every chance. Informed passengers on river and Jeep trips advanced my education. Books and articles recommended to me were secured and read. Each scholar and professional man shared what he could with me. If I led an anthropologist or archaeologist to a special pictograph or petroglyph that had been puzzling me, he would search his own storehouse of facts for clues to its explanation. Geologists and prospectors enlarged my frame of reference for the rocks I loved to study as well as climb upon.

A friend once sent me a geologist's report, ready for

publication, on the Blue and West Mountains. He wanted to know whether my familiarity with the mountains and close observation of the rock would tally with the writer's theory that the mountains are five laccoliths, pushed up into sedimentary Mancos Shale and Morrison Formation. I studied the report carefully and thoroughly. Previous information and similar contacts helped me understand it. Then I went back to the mountains to re-examine the rocks. His paper added to my knowledge. The writer found my facts in agreement with what he wrote.

Opportunities of this kind occurred again and again. Such experiences drew out of me material I had collected from hard observation; reassembling these facts in a new way. I could reach a greater understanding of what I observed.

Randall Henderson recommended me to Dr. H. H. Neininger, a meteorite scientist, as a guide to take him to the Sahara Desert. Dr. Neininger wanted to see a meteor discovered during the war years. An American had taken samples of it and reported it. I made a special trip to Arizona in '57 to see Dr. Neininger. Although he eventually abandoned the trip, I enjoyed several lengthy discussions with him on meteorites. In '63, in the Needles, I astonished my passengers by stopping the Jeep, jumping out, and grabbing a grubby-looking rock that was barely showing in the ground.

"It's a meteorite!" I exclaimed. They kept their excitement under control.

"How do you know?"

"Feel its weight. Look at its composition. Do you see those streaks on it?"

"It looks like just another rock to us," they said coolly.

Dr. Neininger came to our home two weeks later, inspected the rock, and confirmed its authenticity. Then he went on a Jeep trip with me, back to the same spot to look for more. We were unable to find any.

Ruby, our first brand new Jeep purchased after Emmy, turned her 100,000th mile crossing Elephant Hill at nine years of age. This amounted to about 6,000 hours of driving time on my part in Ruby alone, not considering any of our other vehicles. For a dedicated hiker, that's not a bad driving record. Now much older, Ruby is the Cadillac of Jeeps on the road. Naturally she is my favorite. I have rebuilt every part in her from stem to stern and replaced the motor with a more powerful one. My ambition seems to be to keep Ruby going with me.

Except for the replaced motor—which is Ruby's special distinction—I lavish this kind of care on all our carriers. After each trip I go through them all, checking and adjusting and lubricating parts.

In 1964 Fern and I were asked to furnish vehicles and guide a trip into the Needles for a group of 65 businessmen from Salt Lake City. It was a highly successful trip. When Fern reached the top of Elephant Hill on the way back she stopped to let her passengers watch other Jeeps coming up the difficult road, thinking with elation, "My, I feel good." As always, she was the only woman driver. Twenty minutes later she had brought them safely down the other rough side of Elephant Hill and was driving an easy stretch at the bottom when she fainted at the wheel.

From the hospital at Monticello to the hospital in Salt Lake City countless physicians puzzled over what could have caused it. She still had no pain, but they detected a pressure in her head. Two days later they operated and removed a large tumor over the right temple. In spite of the major surgery, she was walking regularly twenty-four hours later and was discharged from the hospital in ten days. Dr. Goon of Monticello introduced her to an intern by saying, "I want you to know this woman has the strength of three men."

Fern's recovery was complete and rapid. She still laughs about the way she confused the earliest diagnoses when she regained consciousness in the Needles. She found herself lying on the ground on a blanket. Several men were hovering over her, asking, "Where does it hurt?"

She pointed to her right foot, saying, "I hurt right there."

What she was feeling was the effect of the tremendous pressure she had exerted on the brake to stop the Jeep at the moment she realized she was not well. The first instincts of a Jeep driver are to avoid trouble.

Chapter 18

Time for solitary hikes became limited, although each January 1 still beckoned. But my hiking habits changed somewhat. I found I could share with others the arduous journey afoot, the unpredictable weather, the silent magnificence of individual discovery . . . those others from the cities who were willing to arrive at a special appreciation earned only the hard way. A few trekked out to backpack with me over old horse and deer trails, into empty canyons, to sleep on cave floors beside campfires.

Dr. Bill was the first. His steam-engine stride set the pace for us in Dark Canyon, a huge corridor of exceptional beauty. Its black limestone inner gorge is a dramatic contrast to the brightly colored sandstone formations above. He came again, and other hikers formed a slim trickle through the years.

Then the Goldmans came from Chicago. The power and beauty of the land had such an impact on them, Rosalie and Mel, that they returned for two more hikes within the year. They had a vast enthusiasm for everything that attracted me. They came the following year for more hikes, and the next and the next.

At first we covered ground that I thought would be a review for me. I took them down Grand Gulch in November. They thrilled to it. Outside my secret kiva we were imagining the busy life that had occupied it a thousand years before.

"What's this?" asked Rosalie. She pulled at something sticking out of the sand on which we sat. Up came a finely woven prehistoric sandal. It has its place in our Monticello museum.

I sent them David Miller's book on the pioneer Hole-in-the-Rock expedition, so that they would be informed for our spring hike over the Mormon Trail of 1880. These places were not new to me, yet the hikes became more discovery than review. Because of the way the Goldmans adapted and appreciated, I was seeing my canyons with someone else's excitement added. They never refused a climb to an interesting view or a ledge with a promise of discovery.

I was inclined to say, "Let's rest our packs," more often than usual. It was not to be expected that Rosalie could maintain the pace of us men. I didn't mind. I was finding that, for the first time, I could observe details in a leisurely way that I had missed on my headlong plunges alone in reverie.

In Lake Canyon we pushed through a tangled barrier of underbrush and counted the scratches worthwhile. It was a pretty canyon, full of fine Indian ruins that were rarely seen. A long-walled structure was reached by ancient steps carved in the rock. Once inside, we looked around, surprised.

"Gourds," we said together, stating the obvious.

Mel picked up one. "It's a foot long, and so are the others."

We started counting, "One, two, three. . . ." There were thirty of them . . . the remains of prehistoric farming. All were hollow, each with one neat hole at the bottom.

"What do you suppose these are?" Rosalie asked. She

was kneeling beside four sockets drilled at the base of the back wall. Smooth bars crossed through them. It had been a loom. I reported this ruin to the University of Utah who sent a crew to do further research.

In a nearby gully I spotted a large, grey basketball. "But," I mused, "there's been no one playing ball here lately." I started to climb down to search for it and found instead a splendid jar in perfect condition. Our concern for getting *it* rather than our supplies out safely set us to condensing our packs to accommodate it. Then we walked miles over the Land of Rock and Sand with it; over hills and hummocks of rock that billow like an ocean. The Goldmans were surprised to find that we could arrive at the Jeep by dead reckoning across this moon country that was utterly lacking in landmarks.

"It's mighty comfortable to be here with you, Kent," they said. "Very few could find their way on foot here."

Ah, the lazy hours we spent on the Colorado's bank, sitting in the spring sunshine, studying Hole-in-the-Rock across the river from us. That was a beautiful trip. My favorite knife came out, and I could hear Grandpa Frost talking as I carved willow whistles in different keys. When our whistle-blowing concert slowed down I said, "Here's something else my grandfather taught me to make." I drew a deerskin slingshot from my pack. Smooth, rounded river stones make good ammunition. One flew across the Colorado River to the opposite shore. A stone's throw.

It drew our attention back to Hole-in-the-Rock. The Hole appeared as a dark slash in the opposite canyon wall. The steep chute was one of the challenges for the pioneers of the 1880 trail.

"I just don't see why they picked such a hard place," said Rosalie.

"Their scouts led them to those cliffs across from us. When they realized the difficulties, it was too late to change," I explained.

The narrow slit running down the perpendicular wall was the pathway for people, wagons, and horses.

"How high are the cliffs, Kent?" Mel asked.

"It's a quarter of a mile down to the river. They camped at the top of the cut. They worked two winter months to widen it and ease the grade."

"Here," I said, handing them the binoculars. "You can see the place where they dynamited a narrow shelf in the solid wall. They built the path out into the air with poles and fill. They grooved the wall to hold the inside wheels and keep the wagons from tipping off."

"It sounds like a marvel of road engineering. What energy," Rosalie said.

"The entire company plunged down that wild incline a wagon at a time on January 26," I said, and then added, "the upper chute was such a tight fit for the wagons that the scrape marks of the hubs are still in the walls today."

"We'll have to get over there and see for ourselves, some day," they decided.

A retired cowboy had told me about a trail he used here twenty years before. I found it the next dawn. On that fresh, early spring morning the Goldmans followed me to the top of a great talus slope that swept 600 feet down to the Colorado. Rising sheer above us were Navajo sandstone walls. The faint trail hugged a Kayenta ledge on top of the talus at the foot of the walls for three miles. We traveled like tiny bugs at the tenth brick of a twenty-brick wall. We passed a cave so rich with life that lovely redbud trees were blooming in it. Cactus was flowering everywhere. As we hiked the shady side of the river we could see the sun breaking onto a sea of rocky red far ahead . . . it was the tops of the canyons around us. Always, straight down, was the river. Small springs appeared. We stopped to channel one into a hole—the flow, about a drop a minute. Mel laughed.

"This is what you call developing a water hole," he said. On our return that night a can of water was waiting for us. At one point the talus pinched in and the trail petered out. It took imagination to believe that a cowboy had talked his cows into going on there.

"This must be where Stevens said he always got off

and walked his horse," I commented. At the end the trail opened out into two miles of sage and rabbit brush meadow, winter pasture in a land of meager forage. A clop of hooves rushed towards us. We had frightened two wild cows, descendants of Stevens' old herd, owned by no one. They ran like race horses, the thinnest cows we ever saw. Beyond the meadow everything came to a point at the confluence of the San Juan and Colorado Rivers, even the two, different-colored, muddy waters.

Major Powell passed this point July 31, 1869. His diary records: "Soon after dinner, we discover the mouth of the San Juan, where we camp. The remainder of the afternoon is given to hunting some way by which we can climb out of the canyon, but it ends in failure." In 1869 he could not climb up to where we were, 93 years later. Nor, in 1961, could we now climb down to where he had landed. We sat on the cliff's edge at the confluence, our feet dangling over.

"What's around the bend, Kent?" they asked. "What's it like to travel down there on the river?"

"That's the start of the most glamorous section of Glen Canyon," I told them. "First you come to Hidden Passage and Music Temple."

"What are they?"

I enjoyed answering their questions about the wonders that lay around the bend there in Glen Canyon. And out of these questions their next trip was born. I also enjoyed their questions on trail-finding, tracking, animals, rocks, vegetation, history. I taught Rosalie to shoot a gun. I showed Mel bobcat, porcupine, and coyote tracks, and he brought down a porcupine from a tree.

I told them no two canyons are alike. Every one I have ever investigated has its own personality, its own secrets. By way of proving it, we then hiked two parallel canyons that share a common wall. Each is so different that it could be on another side of the world. Wilson Creek Canyon has tiny fish in its brooks and small woods along the way, busy with hummingbirds. Old Settler's Canyon on the other side of the same wall is barren and dry, a chain of thousands of spectacular potholes from its head all the way to the San Juan, with nothing to feed a bird or a lizard.

Our next adventure brought me into new territory. In the fall we built a remarkable raft to float through the most glamorous part of Glen Canyon. The raft was made of flotsam and jetsam that I had gathered from the roadside as I drove our Jeep to the Rincon, an abandoned bend of the river. The raft was a collector's triumph when it was finished, tied together with bailing wire and odd bits of dynamite fuse. It floated on four truck inner tubes that we blew up by mouth.

The reason for the raft, instead of a boat, was that it could be abandoned where we chose so that we could finish the journey on foot. It was the idea that our confluence trip had inspired six months before.

The raft and the river trip were delightful. We reluctantly abandoned our odd little craft at the mouth of Forbidden Canyon and hiked to Rainbow Bridge, then out the other side of it into Navajoland.

This section between Navajo Mountain and the San Juan River was new to me. It was exceedingly beautiful and lonesome. The eroded face of Navajo Mountain, brooding over its province, was full of color. The canyons draining down from the mountain to the San Juan —all of which we had to cross—were full of multicolored walls and spines of stone that took on a silvery shine in the faint rains. The mists hung so low we actually walked with our heads in the clouds sometimes.

After several days of travel we finally arrived at one occupied Navajo hogan. We were graciously received. Two beautiful mothers, dressed in velvet, satin, and jewelry, sat on the hogan floor with five children quietly beside them. They spoke no English. One father appeared later. His first question was, "Are you hungry? Can I give you something to eat?"

As we were leaving, after a fine visit, he told us that a daughter far away was a student at the University of Southern California.

We still had the wide, fast San Juan River to ford. It was icy water. I relied on my river experience to choose the best place. I warned Rosalie and Mel. "Lean on your poles against the current. Don't watch the waves." They soon learned why. It makes the watcher dizzy. The best ford I could choose required fifteen minutes to cross. Our feet were numb. We warmed them up in the sun in familiar, verdant Wilson Creek Canyon on the other shore. Wilson brought us up on the Land of Rock and Sand again, and back to our Jeep at the Rincon.

We had completed a remarkable twelve-day circle, but the Jeep needed exercise after sitting waiting for us hikers such a long time. So we turned off at Sunshine Mesa on the way home for some roller-coaster excitement.

The area bubbled with small rock domes. I swung Ruby Jeep around one, gathering up speed to zoom off onto the next. We raced around its perimeter, then veered off to another—circled it, then on to another. Each change of dome sent us spinning in an opposite direction. Sometimes the Jeep was careening at close to 40 degree angle.

"Wheeeee," they sang.

"Darn good maneuvering, Kent," grinned Mel.

"What fun," glowed Rosalie, "let's do it again."

It was hard to quit and go home.

"Hair-raising adventure" describes the time I led Mel, Rosalie, and their son, Glenn, through White Canyon Narrows. The Narrows is an inner gorge, barely three feet wide in many sections, with sheer walls that rise hundreds of feet. Its still-standing pools are deep and cold in the gloom of the bottom, where sunshine rarely touches.

In July, in swimsuits, we waited hours at the head of the Narrows for the red flood water to subside. We needed the flood water to warm up the pools, ordinarily too cold to endure. But we didn't need so much of it in that tight region.

When the time seemed right, about 11:30 A.M., we

Tortuous, intriguing White Canyon when floodwater is running.

climbed down over an active waterfall into the murky, winding passage, intending to swim through any pools too deep for wading. Unexpectedly, the pouring falls and racing water were churning up a red foam that piled over the surface and could not be beaten down. It was several feet high and produced a toxic effect on us when we got our faces in it. Our eyes burned, our throats choked. We could not survive it. Swimming was out of the question. The foam was higher than our heads.

Four of us crowded into a tiny alcove built for one and stood shivering, trying to think. They were good people to share a trying situation with. Since at that moment they didn't have any plans they thought worth mentioning, they said nothing and gave me time to think it over. We were so cold that our teeth were chattering audibly.

I had brought along one tiny air mattress. Inflating it, I took an experimental ride from our alcove to the next bend, paddling with my hands. With extreme caution it was possible to balance on it. I picked up a passenger, ferried him to the next shallow stand-up station, then returned for another. We had to repeat this operation over and over, to maneuver through one deep, foam-covered pool after another for hours and hours.

We were cold, cold, cold, in our wet bathing suits, with no chance to dry out. No sun to warm us a little bit, no chance even to be very active. It was night when White Canyon's walls finally opened out into a normal canyon again. We had come a brief distance of perhaps two miles.

We still had a difficult climb to get out of the canyon. The small piece of rope I was carrying proved too short to be useful on one slick rock chute. I added my belt to it to get the right length. We dragged ourselves back to camp by starlight. No one wanted to eat or drink. We sank gratefully on the ground and slept until a welcome, hot morning sun opened our eyes; it was the first time we had felt warm since 11:30 A.M. the previous day. It is the only trip we would not care to repeat.

CHAPTER 19

Before or after most of our trips there were opportunities to introduce Rosalie and Mel to local residents. Their understanding of this special part of the country grew as they met my relatives, townspeople, cowboys, river men, tradespeople, officials, and specialized workers with whom I associated.

We watched young Irwin Oliver rope and brand some lively cattle on Elk Mountain, then went on with him to meet his family at his mountain ranch home. We visited with some sheepherders in Standing Rocks. The Goldmans met Hite's first ferry operator, Art Chaffin, and later met its last, Woody Edgel. They met the Moab widow whose cave home had been carved out with dynamite, a room at a time, by her husband. They met Hazel Ekker whose girlhood at the family ranch in Robbers' Roost meant knowing outlaws. Some were celebrities, most were pleasant, ordinary folk; a few were exaggerated personalities.

I could not have expected, however, the character that

floated our way the day after our White Canyon adventure. As we drove along Highway 95 we came to the bustling activity of the Happy Jack Mine. It was one of the most successful mines of the uranium boom which was drawing to a close.

As we stood watching the mine cars slide from the tunnel and dump their loads, he came up beside us. On that hot day he was wearing a wool shirt with his blue jeans. His long grey hair was straight and hung down to his shoulders. It was almost as long in front and hung heavily over his face. That the arrangement of his hair was deliberate grooming and not accidental was apparent from the way he removed his wide-brimmed hat. He took it off straight up and put it on straight down, as though he did not wish to muss a single hair. You could tell where his ears were by the bulges they made in his hair. Soon we were talking.

"You won't see this much longer," he offered. "Mining's almost ending here. Hardly any use for me to prospect any more."

He was also an ex-trapper, we soon learned. He had spent the major portion of his life alone in these empty places. Too late for him to return to the society of the town. He watched Glenn peel off his shirt. We were standing in the sun.

"After yesterday," said Glenn, "I just want that sun to shine on me."

"I been cold often enough, too, sonny," agreed our friend, "to always appreciate it when the sun shines. That's why I always buy wool shirts. This here shirt's my new one. Every fall when I get to town I buy the best shirt I can get. It goes on under my old one. If I come in again at Christmas, I get another. That, being the newest, goes on under the fall shirt. Winter's cold, and I can be warmer in all three shirts. When spring comes, and the weather warms up considerable, off comes my outside shirt. That's the oldest, so I throw it away. Last week weather warmed up enough so I took off the next shirt and threw it away."

We stayed on and on, discussing trapping and prospecting with him. He turned to me.

"What's your work?" When I told him, he said, "I did some of that myself, a long time ago. Never did own my own outfit. Just helped vacation ranches that took dudes on pack trips. It was a darn long, hard trip in those days to bring a party of people way down here. No road like this 95 to travel."

"I know," I said, "I hiked along here to Hite before the road was built."

"Then you know," he continued, "they couldn't pack in enough supplies. If they didn't shoot enough deer, the party might get a bit hongry.

"Oncet, there was a young feller for cook. He used to mix biscuits for dinner right in his flour sack, just working the top of the flour. The customers was particularly hongry one evening. They didn't get any lunch that day. One grabbed a biscuit from the top of the sack and swallered it raw. Then another got the idea and did the same thing. Before he could say anything, hands was reaching into his flour bag from all directions and grabbing for biscuits. Everybody grabbing exasperated the young feller. Seems like he just felt the situation getting away from him.

" 'Next one that puts his hand in that bag is going to have it shot off,' he sputtered. There's always someone to pick up a tease like that. I was standing right there when one of the men reached into the bag to take another.

" 'All right,' he shouts, 'you asked for it!' Whips out his pistol quick as anything and fires right into the man's hand."

Our friend had Glenn's complete attention by then. Any other "young feller" has a special appreciation of such a situation.

"What happened then?" Glenn asked, as the old man seemed to think his tale was over.

"We rushed the wounded man to Blanding by wagon. He had a bad hand."

"And the cook?" persisted Glenn.

"Being essential, he continued with the group. There warn't no further interference. Everyone respected him as a man of his word."

That story had top priority as a campfire tale for a long, long time. "Put your gun away, Kent," said Rosalie on our next trip. "While you're mixing biscuits in the top of your flour bag. We just might want to grab some raw ones."

I was taking her and their daughter, Nell, down the Escalante River while Mel was taking his sons, Don and Glenn, on the wild Grand Canyon run. Nell was ten and too young for those rapids. But the adventures she had to cope with on our Escalante trip turned out to be the equal of what she might have faced in Grand Canyon, if slightly different in character.

Escalante Canyon was unknown to me; it was a place I was eager to see and had not yet had the time to explore. El Toro looked like a mighty small orange Jeep out there in the absolute desert thirty miles from the nearest town, parked at the edge of billowing rock castles. There was a strange quality of expectancy to the canyon from the moment we entered, summed up by Nell's remark, "I think the canyon wants to show us surprises."

It was attractive from the moment of entrance and grew more so. Temperatures were over 100° every day, but we soaked ourselves in the Escalante River flowing at the canyon's bottom. We hiked until we were dry—perhaps half an hour—then we soaked again, with our clothes on, even tennis shoes. No need for sleeping bags in that heat. We left them at the Jeep. Anything that lightens the pack lightens the step. We slept on the bare ground beside the fire, and our steps were light.

There is a fairy tale quality to that canyon. Escalante is sliced from beautiful rock that has been sculptured on a grand scale. Every side canyon conceals an arch or cave or vault in sandstone colors of cream, beige, salmon, pink, and brown. The bottom is gentle and generous, with green plants, willows, and cottonwood trees beside the river.

The strange quality of promise that hung in the air fulfilled itself each day at lovely Hamblin Arch in Coyote Gulch, mighty Stevens Arch on the skyline,

Coyote Natural Bridge, the awesome hall of Cathedral-in-the-Desert, Broken Bow Arch in Willow Springs. There are few places with more gifts to give.

Nell proved to be such a good little hiker with her tiny back pack that we extended our trip to reach the Colorado River instead of climbing out at Willow Creek. This meant short rations and added days.

It was fun to work it out. I shot a duck on the wing for our dinner one night. Another night I shot twelve frogs in a pond. Twelve pairs of frog legs (24 for three people), plus one perch and one sucker, cooked for supper beside exquisite Gregory Arch. A desert fox barked at us half the night, scolding us for taking his cave. We stopped often to crowd over our map and count Escalante's bends until the next side canyon.

All three of us stepped over a rattlesnake without knowing it when we explored a narrow gorge in Willow Creek. He was sleeping under a rock, and raised his head after we passed. I shot him and was ready to kick his corpse aside. I don't treasure snakes. But to the ladies this was one more delightful adventure, and they wanted the skin.

"You can have it if you skin him and cure it."

"Just tell us how," they said. So, bright-eyed as though they were slicing up angel food cake, they cut off the skin and mopped up the moisture with paper, while the denuded snake continued to writhe on the ground in front of them. Then they sprinkled salt over the inside of the skin and took turns working it in their hands for the rest of the day as we ambled along. That snakeskin is in *their* museum in Chicago, where it can stay.

Somehow, as though it had been washed down there for us—the nearest community was sixty miles away—an inner tube lay in the river. I brought it along to the Colorado beach. To it I tied a driftwood log. The ties were willow sapling, cut with the same old knife. I also carved a few small pieces of driftwood into paddles. It was a make-believe raft, but we didn't have far to go.

"All aboard." We shoved off for a dreamy four-mile float through Glen Canyon and landed at Hole-in-the-

Rock. From the river bottom, it used to be a 2,000-foot climb. At the last spring on the trail, close to the bottom, we drank all the water we could hold, filled our one-quart canteen, and started up that historic old pathway. Danced up it might be more accurate, as the hot rocks burned through the soles of tennis shoes on that scorching, high-summer afternoon. We still managed to pause to observe the remarkable remains of the 1880 route and the scars left in the rocks by the wagon hubs.

We rested for two hours at the top, where it was over 100 degrees in the shade. As the sun set behind Kaiparowitz Plateau, I told the girls, "We won't be any hotter out there than we are here. Let's start hiking that desert." We were twenty-five miles from the Jeep, in the middle of an empty land with no water. A night hike was dictated. There would be no relief in the day. The stars came out. The land cooled off. We tramped up- and downhill as the road headed up one after another of the canyons that came down from Kaiparowitz.

At 11 P.M. Nell bent down and picked up a small horseshoe that lay in the road in front of her. She kept it in her hand. As she walked ever more slowly, we coaxed her to let us carry it for her; but she did not want to let it go, although its extra weight was burdening her. Finally she was willing to make a wish, spit on the horseshoe, and toss it over her left shoulder. But even though she was relieved of the horseshoe, she was too tired after nine miles of hiking to go any farther.

We stopped at Soda Gulch Ranch, which was unoccupied in the summer. I had counted on finding a spring there. The spring was dry. It was now urgent for me to reach the Jeep by morning. Leaving the girls at the roadside at midnight with cowboy wood for a fire, I hiked the rest of the night without slowing down (except for occasional sleepwalking, when stumbling would awaken me). Pale light was spreading in the east as I passed by Dance Hall Rock. I had not found any drinkable water all night. But this landmark meant I was nearing the ridge that would lead me to the Jeep. At 7:30 A.M. I stumbled wearily across the last knob of sandstone to reach

El Toro Jeep. Water. Transportation. As soon as I drank my fill I started driving right back down the road.

A sympathetic feeling gripped me as I saw my weaving footsteps of last night in the dust before me all along the way. Two happy females hailed me from the roadside.

"We just lost the last bit of shade." "What good timing." "How tired you must be, Kent." "My, how wonderful water tastes," in between gurgles of water. I noted on the speedometer that I had walked 26½ miles that night, and the girls had managed a considerable share themselves.

Yes, I was tired. But first we had to return to the head of the Hole for our packs. On the way I slowed the Jeep to a crawl, leaned out from my steering wheel, swept something from the road, and handed it to Nell—her horseshoe.

The only shade on that whole desert was under the Jeep, so that's where I crawled for a few hours' sleep.

The Escalante trip went on for twenty splendid days. Escalante is one of Utah's charming towns (Boulder and Teasdale are two other favorites). Each home is centered in a large piece of property that invariably has a truck garden, flower garden, stable, corral, and sometimes place of business. The desert stands at the town's limits, with a mountain behind and the river flowing through.

"How would you like to meet the cousin who helped me through school?" I asked Rosalie and Nell. We had several visits with Clara, as we used Escalante for our headquarters for a while and explored out from it. Clara, now a married woman with beautiful children, had not lost any of her knack of being helpful. She gave us produce from her garden and six fresh-caught rainbow trout. She cringed at the snakeskin. Her family arranged for our visit to Escalante's unusual museum and urged us to explore Spooky Gulch back on the desert. We did it all—and more. Taking a cut through Kaiparowitz, we wound up at the smoking pots on Collett Top, where an underground fire in a coal vein sends hot gases and smoke up through cracks in the rocks. A drive down Last Chance Canyon brought us to a splendid top-of-the-cliffs lookout over the Colorado River, where we picked up—sea shells! We viewed one of the great sunsets of a lifetime that evening. Active rain clouds were dragging bright red streamers of rain to distant ground. The air was filled with dust which turned a fiery red near us. That was my longest trip, and almost every bit of it was new territory for me; it was all a happy time.

Conquering new territory with the Goldmans came to be a habit. As I recalled old wishes and curiosities, I recalled Kanab Canyon. In my days of river running we once had beached at its mouth. Kanab starts in Utah and drops south through Arizona to meet Grand Canyon. Mel, Rosalie, and I entered Kanab through its side canyon, Hacks. Kanab turned out to be a rugged, exciting place, its bottom choked with house-sized boulders at the lower end. It also has a permanent stream. Its giant sheer walls that closed in on a narrow corridor were pink. Kanab Creek produced hanging gardens of wild orchids, travertine waterfalls, and cavernous overhangs.

As big and rough as Kanab was, our subsequent hike in Grand Canyon was rougher. We had planned only nine days and had not included Grand Canyon. But to arrive at the mightiest place of them all—with so much effort—and not to take advantage of it, was unthinkable. So we extended our stay to thirteen days and proceeded upcanyon to Thunder Falls and Tapeats Creek; the walls of Grand Canyon, towering a mile above our heads, were covered with snow.

We tightened our belts and started "living off the land."

"The living is good," said Mel, carrying a watermelon-sized barrel cactus to place on the coals beside six fat carp that were roasting there. Then we picked wild watercress along Deer Creek there in Surprise Valley for our salad. Mormon tea brewed a fine hot drink for us. There is no end to what the land is willing to furnish people if they are willing to compromise a bit.

The one thing I have always dreaded is the possibility of being rescued unnecessarily. I always told Fern, "Wait at least two days before you send any search parties after me." We were more than two days late now. I had a qualm or two about whether, as we emerged hale and healthy over the rim of Kanab, we would meet an anxious posse out looking for us.

Once, on our raft-hike trip through Glen Canyon, we had set fire to a giant cache of driftwood in Cottonwood Canyon. That is a fine way to have a great bonfire. The heat was so intense that big boulders were cracking and banging in the fire throughout the night. The next morning, as we launched our raft and got ready to leave the beach, an airplane spotted the heavy smoke still rising from the fire's ashes and came circling down about us.

"Don't look up," I had said, "don't wave. Let's just get this raft into the water and go." The plane left us without further concern on that occasion.

This time, as we emerged from Kanab, I was relieved to find that no one was looking for us. We appreciated our unpublicized return.

Off on a hill of its own, an arch so unique I named it —Beehive.

CHAPTER 20

The Maze. Whoever named it knew it. Every time I brought a party into Standing Rocks I knew it was there, sunken from view. It was an unexplored tangle of canyons whose tops barely showed. There were tantalizing bits I could observe from here and there, where they came to dead ends at the edge of the Land of Standing Rocks. How to get in and have an exploring good time there? The best way seemed to be by entering from the river side.

"How would you like to build another raft and float down Green River this time?" I asked the Goldmans. "We can try to enter The Maze through the mouth of one of its canyons." They thought that was a wonderful idea. Spring found us assembling such a raft at Mineral Canyon on the Green River. The water was low when we started. But each day the river rose steadily with the spring runoff.

Two men were working on a water pump at Anderson Bottom. They were amazed at our float when we pulled ashore to chat with them. It was actually a sturdier, safer little craft than their flimsy outboard, but they weren't accustomed to such sights.

Doc Tangreen, a veteran cowman from Moab, muttered, "Never thought I'd see a woman come down the river on a thing like that. I'd say it was good way to get rid of her."

The river was fine and scenic, but we could not enter The Maze. We reached the juncture of the Green with the Colorado and were still down below, looking up at the walls we wished we could mount.

One more bend of the river would toss us into the first rapids of Cataract Canyon. It was absolutely time to stop. Spanish Bottom was there on our right. We beached our craft twenty feet above the shoreline, tied it securely to willows, again drank all the water we could hold, and climbed the Spanish Stairs.

It was twenty-four hours before we had another drink; that was the longest we ever went without water. We got it from a small pothole—in The Maze! I had found a way in. We were launched in the East Maze for the first of many explorations of an absorbing area. There was one practical, intricate route that crossed valleys and included several passages through crevices. I happened to hit every one of them. We worked our way from canyon to canyon, investigating all tributaries along the way. Our heads were awhirl with the treasures we were finding.

"There's so much to see. We can never do it all on one trip," said Rosalie. She was right. They returned three more times, and I made solitary trips of my own in between. The ancient Indians had lived all over it. Their chips were everywhere. For once they had not had to carry the heavy rock from elsewhere. Great ledges of beautiful jasper lay exposed in many places.

The pioneer stockmen had also been there. "Even those rugged men found it too hard," I said, when we came to the last of their old trail work. There were still good canyons beyond, so they must have given up in discouragement at such a complicated place. The Butch

Cassidy gang is also supposed to have used The Maze as a hideaway.

One of the oddest features of the East Maze was Jasper Highway. On the second day I discovered a shelf, about halfway up a canyon wall, that linked all the canyons. It continued like a road from one canyon to its neighbor. It was literally paved with hundreds of thousands of red and purple jasper chips. Chips only. We never found a single tool. The Fremont Indians, while traveling Jasper Highway, had practiced great economy. They carried out everything they made.

The East Maze is splattered with natural arches. We discovered at least one a day. We even came face to face with a single wall perforated by two noteworthy arches. Off in the corner of another side canyon, where we almost missed it, was a large arch shaped like a funnel or megaphone. A tiny boxcar rock with a square window in it was perched on a great dividing wall and could be reached only by strenuous climbing. Peering through the window, we had a nice view of the country and of the Green River, 2,000 feet below. One charming arch, set off on a hill of its own, had a shape so unique that I decided to name it Beehive Arch. It is well suited to its home state of Utah, whose symbol is the beehive. Washington, D.C. accepted "Beehive Arch" officially. I also officially named a canyon in the Maze, "Defiance Canyon."

The days of wandering along in a lonesome land and calling a topographical feature what you please are gone. That method of naming lasts only while a scant few souls wander an area and are glad to pick up something offered by a previous human being. I named a number of places that way in my earlier exploring days, including the Silver Stairs. But now if one wants to label a location he must do it formally. I am not eager to splash names around the remaining few wild canyons, but once in a while a name helps a person find his way.

I think the old cowboy, Indian, and Spanish names of former generations were more appropriate and colorful than most of today's. Who can improve on The Golden Stairs, Land of Standing Rocks, Sunset Pass, Owachomo Bridge, The Great Goosenecks, Lavender Butte, Six-Shooter Peaks, The Maze, Robbers' Roost, Comb Ridge, Jacob's Chair, Fable Valley, Navajo Baby, Rainbow Bridge, Beef Basin, Colorado River?

But in The Maze we no longer mused about naming places when we observed that our supplies were at a new low. The last waterholes were drying up fast. The Maze was not being very hospitable. We knew it was time to get out and return to the raft. As we reached the top of the Spanish Stairs, storm clouds broke. It was raining in The Maze—too late to do us any good. At Spanish Bottom our raft (left twenty feet up on dry land) was floating. The river was still rising. We had to cross and land at Red Lake Canyon or unwillingly take our handmade raft over the rapids of Cataract Canyon. The paddles splashed hard in midstream. We made it with about a sixth of a mile to spare and immediately hiked down to see the rapids we had just cheated.

A deer trail took us up the many rough ridges of Red Lake Canyon, a beautiful place with a limestone layer full of crinoids, brachiopods, and many other fossils of ancient sea life that had been deposited there several hundred million years ago. It was queer to see the Jeep waiting in Cyclone Canyon in the Needles, where Fern had left it for us. After Spartan living, Jeep camping offered so many comforts that it made life seem unusually rich. On the Jeep's seat was a new brochure, just published by our National Parks Bureau in Washington, with a note from Fern saying, "Read page 10."

Page 10 said, "The Maze—as yet unexplored—is fascinating wilderness."

And we had just explored it! We were the first.

Pete's Mesa splits The Maze in two. We explored the West Maze a year later. It was different from its mate, with wider floors, more water, occasional pictographs, and very few arches. One pictograph was exceptional. We found it one morning as we entered an arena in which several canyons met.

"What a beautiful wall," said Mel. We all turned our heads to admire the sweeping curve of smooth pale rock. Then we stopped, silent at our simultaneous discovery.

The ancient Indians must also have admired that wall. They had chosen it for a masterful display of paintings in three colors.

"This is no hodge-podge accumulation of passing doodlers," Mel observed. "It's a planned composition."

It is. The huge panel has deliberate grouping and design. The portraits are heroic size. Mel was measuring himself against the height of the central figures. "At least eight feet." Many small ones in the background create perspective.

A regal figure holds a tree in his hand while the animals of the land parade past. Another bends over with a forked stick as though water witching. Action drawings like this are rare in prehistoric paintings.

We camped nearby so that we could make return visits to our newly discovered gallery.

Each visit to The Maze convinced us all that we must return again. The canyon I ultimately named Defiance was a challenge to me for years. It was a sheer-walled box canyon up against Pete's Mesa. It foiled every attempt at entry. I thought I had tried it from all approaches until I located a side canyon that almost admitted me. One lip of rock overhung a twenty-foot wall that I could negotiate, if I could get to it.

"I could return with climber's gear, or . . . ," I speculated. In a few weeks I came back alone with the "or"—six sticks of dynamite. I dug a small channel above the lip, placed the six sticks of dynamite end to end in it, and covered them deeply with dirt. My fuse was short, about a foot long. So, after lighting it, I scrambled to the cover of a protective rock, 200 feet away. A few seconds later the canyon suddenly filled with the thunder of blasting dynamite. Rocks rolled and tumbled to the ledges below. After the dust settled I hurried over. The three-foot lip of rock was completely gone for a space of six feet. I cleaned out the debris and climbed down, cutting sev-

The gallery—a splendid wall of ancient pictographs we discovered in The Maze.

eral Moqui steps with my hammer. In twenty minutes I was at the bottom of the canyon that was so important to me. As I walked along in wonder and triumph I found several Indian spearheads and skinning knives out in the open. Had anyone else been here, they would have removed them. So perhaps I was the first. The desert moss was completely unbroken. The only traces of animal life were those of lizards and tiny creatures.

Apparently not even the deer had been able to come in here successfully. The undisturbed character of the desert moss indicated that. I could not locate any deer trails. Everything I saw, including Indian caves near a verdant spring, was untouched. It would seem that I was the first man in modern times to enter. The thrill was very great. And I officially named it "Defiance Canyon," approved by Washington, D.C.

I had always said that a person has to have rocks in his head to carry out rocks in his backpack. But I did it in Defiance. Like the East Maze, it was brimming over with jasper, some of it worked by the prehistoric people. I had to bring back a souvenir of this discovery, so I picked up a fine piece that weighed ten pounds and carried it out. Months later I found another way into Defiance, using pitons and climbing rope, but I have not yet found a third.

The Maze country is a separate world, as the Needles country once was. There are no more vast unexplored areas like that. But there are still lovely little-known canyons and mesa tops that ought to keep me busy for years, when I find time to go see them: the tributaries of Dark Canyon and Gypsum Canyon, Bridger Jack Mesa and Wooden Shoe Mesa and the Jacob's Chair area.

I intend to try all the boating I can, and to look into caves and coves as I fish and climb. While travel to the cities and countries of our friends appeals to Fern and me, I shall always want to return quickly to this unusual land for the greatest beauty.

For the biggest views, the brilliant edges of dark, rolling storm clouds, the continual rainbows, the sunlight reflected on rainbow-hued rock walls, I shall come here.

Here, where I can stand in silent air under a starry sky watching the lightning show of a storm that's so far away the thunder never reaches me.

I shall always be able to find some empty corner where I can quietly observe the brilliance of the stars at night, smell the perfume of the sage, cedar, and pine in the air or in my fire, and observe the lives of all the birds, animals, and insects interweaving around me.